Conspiracy Theories Unveiled

Exposing the Hidden Truths Behind the 27 Most Controversial Secrets You Can't Ignore

Logan Cross

RIVANNA
HEIGHTS
— MEDIA —

ALSO BY RIVANNA HEIGHTS MEDIA

Pickleball Made Simple by Blake Foster

The Complete Beginner's Guide To ChatGPT by Ryan Harper

Cryptocurrency Investing 101 by Jordan Taylor

CONTENTS

Claim Your Free One-Pager: 9 Mind-Blowing Conspiracy Theories!

As a thank you for purchasing this book, I'm offering you a special bonus: a free one-pager that explores some of the most fascinating and bizarre conspiracy theories people believe.

Inside this one-pager, you'll find:

Celebrity Doppelgängers: Discover which stars are rumored to be replaced by look-alikes.

Secret Lives of Icons: Theories about famous figures who may have faked their deaths.

Global Mysteries: Uncover the wild story about a country that might not even exist.

Get your free one-pager now by clicking or scanning the QR code:

INTRODUCTION

IN 1971, A MAN calling himself D.B. Cooper hijacked a Boeing 727, extorted $200,000 in ransom, and parachuted into the night, never to be seen again. This wasn't just some bold criminal act—it was the beginning of a legacy that would ignite one of the most intense waves of conspiracy theories in modern history. Was Cooper a rogue CIA agent? Did he survive the jump and vanish with the help of the government? Or, as many suspect, did the FBI cover up the truth? D.B. Cooper didn't just disappear—he became the symbol of everything we don't know about the world that's been built behind closed doors.

This book, *Conspiracy Theories Unveiled*, isn't here to play by the rules. It's here to cut through the fog of official lies and expose the hidden truth behind some of the most significant conspiracies of our time. From the secret corridors of the New World Order to the tragedy of 9/11, the Moon Landing Hoax, and UFO cover-ups, we are diving into the deepest, most controversial *theories* that have left generations questioning reality. We're not just examining stories; we're pulling at the strings of a much darker web of manipulation, hidden agendas, and the lengths governments will go to keep us in the dark.

Why? Because understanding conspiracy theories isn't just about curiosity anymore—it's about survival in a world where deception is the standard. These theories aren't fringe beliefs anymore. They shape public opinion, drive political actions, and even fracture personal relationships. The truth is, we're already living in a world molded by these secrets and lies, and it's time to expose how deep it all goes.

I'm Logan Cross, and I've spent years studying the intricate maze of conspiracies that define our modern world. My background in psychology and history isn't just some academic stamp—it's my way of navigating the smoke and mirrors to uncover what's really going on behind closed doors. I wrote this book to give you the real tools to understand why we've been lied to and, more importantly, how to break free from the web of deception we've all been caught in.

Let me make one thing clear right now—I'm not interested in playing the debunker here. That's not what this book is about. This is about tearing down the illusion that's been built brick by brick to keep you complacent, obedient, and blind to the real machinations happening behind the scenes.

This isn't your average conspiracy theory book, and I'm not your average conspiracy theorist. I'm not here to placate you with "balanced" arguments. We're getting straight to the heart of the darkest, most well-guarded secrets that governments and elites have kept from us for generations. And guess what? It's not all theory—much of it is based on hard evidence that they've tried to sweep under the rug. If you think *they* haven't been hiding things from you, you haven't been paying attention. And you will see me use "they" a lot in this book. When you hear it, think about the elite, the powerful, the secretive. The people and the groups that are able to conceal facts from the public without question. This is *they*.

In this book, we're going to explore the real evidence the powerful elite don't want you to see. Sure, we'll glance at the so-called "debunkings," but let's be real—they've been controlling the narrative since day one. The truth is hidden in plain sight, and if you have the courage to look closer, you'll see it too. I'm not here to tell you what to believe; I'm here to show you just how deep the rabbit hole goes—and trust me, it's deeper than you've ever imagined.

You're going to need more than just curiosity on this journey—you're going to need a *Conspiracy Theory Toolbox*. This isn't just a critical thinking exercise; it's a survival kit. I'll arm you with the skills to dissect every headline, every government press release, every official statement with the precision of a surgeon. You'll learn how to spot false flags, recognize when you're being played, and most importantly, how to stay one step ahead of the lies they're feeding us.

So, buckle up. By the time you've finished reading this book, you'll never look at the world the same way again. You'll start to see the patterns, the connections, the hidden hand pulling the strings of every major event that's shaped our modern world. And guess what? Once you start down this road, there's no turning back. You'll become part of a movement that's been growing quietly in the shadows—truth-seekers who refuse to be silenced by the powers that be.

Are you ready for the truth? Because once we start, there's no going back.

CHAPTER 1

THE FOUNDATIONS OF CONSPIRACY THEORIES

IN THE EARLY 2000S, a man named Gary McKinnon hacked into 97 U.S. military and NASA computers. He claimed to have discovered evidence of a secret government program involving UFO technology and free energy suppression. While many dismissed his claims as the ramblings of a determined hacker, others saw a glimpse into hidden truths. This incident underscores the pervasive allure of conspiracy theories and the lengths people will go to reveal or conceal them.

What is a Conspiracy Theory?

At its core, a conspiracy theory is an alternative explanation for events that challenges the official narrative. It operates on the belief that a small, powerful group is pulling the strings behind the scenes, orchestrating significant events to suit their hidden agendas. For those who embrace these theories, the accepted explanations are not only insufficient but are often part of the very conspiracy itself—a deliberate attempt to keep the public blind to the truth. This isn't just speculation, though. Many believe that the very fact that these theories are dismissed by mainstream sources is proof of their legitimacy.

The essence of a conspiracy theory is the secret plot—an intricate game of chess played by powerful forces, unseen by most but with unmistakable consequences. Governments, corporations, shadowy secret societies—these are the players who manipulate events for their gain. The public? Merely pawns in a game they don't even know is being played. And when information is concealed or redacted, conspiracy theorists don't see it as mere bureaucratic oversight—they see it as part of a deliberate effort to keep the truth locked away.

Conspiracy theories thrive in this environment of secrecy, offering alternative explanations that are far more compelling than the dull, watered-down official stories. Take a closer look at the events that have shaped history, and you'll find gaps, inconsistencies, and contradictions that only seem to add fuel to the fire. Whether it's political cover-ups, technological advancements kept under wraps, or historical events that seem too convenient to be accidents, these theories challenge the mainstream narratives and invite us to consider what lies beneath the surface.

The appeal? It's not just about curiosity—it's about control. In a world where chaos reigns, the idea that a few powerful hands are steering the ship can be strangely reassuring. Even if those hands are sinister, at least someone is in control, right? And for those in the know, for those who have peeled back the layers of deception, there's a sense of superiority—of holding secret knowledge that the rest of the population isn't even aware exists. It's the ultimate empowerment: knowing the truth when everyone else is being fed lies.

The conspiracy theory community, built around shared beliefs in hidden plots, offers a refuge. It's a place where like-minded individuals can share their discoveries and explore one another's views without the judgment of the outside world. Conspiracy theories, in a way, foster a sense of belonging—a fellowship united by the quest for truth in a world of deception.

Whether you're looking at political conspiracies like the Watergate scandal or JFK's assassination, scientific ones like the suppression of UFO evidence, or societal control mechanisms that point toward secret societies, each theory offers a different lens through which to view the world. These are more than just stories—they're invitations to challenge everything you've been told, to question the status quo, and to keep your eyes open to the possibility that nothing is as it seems.

As you explore these theories, the key is to maintain a skeptical, yet open, mindset. It's not about blindly accepting every claim—it's about exploring the evidence, questioning the motives, and realizing that the truth, more often than not, is hidden in plain sight. In this world of conspiracy theories, the adventure isn't just about discovering the "what" or the "how"—it's about understanding why these hidden narratives persist and what they reveal about the world we live in.

Welcome to a journey of discovery—where the veil of illusion is lifted, and the real stories begin to emerge. Whether you become a believer or remain skeptical, one thing is certain: after this, you'll never see the world the same way again.

The Historical Roots of Conspiracy Theories

Conspiracy theories are far from modern inventions—they've been woven into the very fabric of human history. For centuries, hidden plots and covert actions have captivated our imaginations and seeded distrust. Let's take a journey through time and expose how these theories have evolved, from whispered secrets to global movements.

The assassination of Julius Caesar in 44 B.C. is one of the earliest conspiracy theories that still resonates today. Was it just a political assassination, or was there a deeper conspiracy involving more than just a few senators? Rome was rife with political intrigue, and it didn't take long for rumors to spread, suggesting that powerful players behind the scenes were orchestrating Caesar's demise to seize control of the Republic. Power, secrecy, betrayal—it was a setup straight out of today's conspiracy playbook.

Fast forward to the Middle Ages, where Europe was consumed by the fear of witchcraft and secret societies. These weren't just isolated accusations of witches; they were massive movements of paranoia, with people claiming that underground forces were manipulating everything from religious decisions to royal courts. The Knights Templar, a Christian military order, found themselves at the center of many of these conspiracies, accused of wielding secret power and knowledge so dangerous it led to their destruction. Were they truly victims of religious persecution, or were they part of a shadowy elite pulling the strings?

Then came the Enlightenment—a period of progress, right? Wrong. It was also a time when secret societies like the Freemasons were rumored to be controlling world events. The Freemasons, who shrouded themselves in rituals and symbols, were believed by many to be orchestrating a New World Order. Were they really just a fraternity of intellectuals, or were they plotting to control governments, economies, and the future of civilization itself? To this day, the Freemasons remain the subject of numerous conspiracies, with their meetings held behind closed doors, leaving the rest of us to wonder what's really going on.

Major historical events only fueled the flames of conspiracy. The French Revolution, far from being a spontaneous uprising, was believed by many to be orchestrated by the Illuminati—a secret society rumored to have manipulated the revolution to establish their rule. Were the Illuminati actually pulling the strings to dismantle monarchies and control societies from behind the curtain? In times of upheaval, it's all too easy to believe there's a mastermind behind the chaos.

The 19th century saw the assassination of Abraham Lincoln, and guess what? Theories abounded. Sure, we all know John Wilkes Booth pulled the trigger, but was he the lone actor? Many theorists suggest otherwise, claiming high-level involvement from Confederate sympathizers or even insiders in Lincoln's own administration. His death wasn't just a tragedy; it was the perfect breeding ground for speculation.

And the 20th century? Conspiracy theories skyrocketed during the world wars. Espionage, covert alliances, secret bases—people couldn't help but wonder who was truly pulling the strings behind these global conflicts. Theories about Nazi occult practices, Soviet infiltration, and secret governmental operations filled the airwaves and the public's imagination. Wars weren't just about countries fighting; they were about global elites playing chess with human lives.

This is the nature of conspiracy theories. They arise in times of instability, feeding on the political and social fears of the time. And guess what? The explosion of media only made them grow. From the invention of the printing press to the rise of the internet, every new form of communication gave these theories a bigger platform to spread.

Conspiracy theories aren't just relics of the past—they're embedded in the DNA of human civilization. Whenever there's power, there's always a plot. And if history tells us anything, it's that the truth is almost always hidden behind closed doors. It's our job to keep questioning, keep digging, and uncover what's really going on.

Let's get one thing straight—when it comes to conspiracy theories, the human brain isn't just some passive observer. No, our minds are wired to dive deep into these narratives, connecting dots that others might miss. Why? Because there are psychological mechanisms at work that make us seek out hidden truths.

One of the biggest culprits here is **confirmation bias**. This isn't just some fancy psychological term—it's the way our minds desperately cling to what we already believe. If you think the government is hiding UFOs, then guess what? You're going to interpret every ambiguous scrap of information as proof. The internet? It's a confirmation bias machine. Social media platforms amplify these beliefs by creating **echo chambers**—places where only your side of the story gets heard. You won't see the other side, and that's exactly why these theories thrive.

But that's not all. Our brains are hardwired for **pattern recognition**—a survival trait from way back when. This trait helps us make sense of a chaotic world. The problem? Sometimes, we start seeing patterns where none exist. Those seemingly disconnected events? They get woven into a larger conspiracy, a grand narrative that feels too compelling to ignore. Think of it as your mind connecting the dots on a cosmic conspiracy chalkboard.

Then, there's **agency detection**. This is our tendency to believe that nothing happens by chance. When big events rock our world—whether it's a terrorist attack, a financial crash, or a natural disaster—it's tough to accept that it could all be random. We search for the hidden hand, the mastermind. And when you look hard enough, it's easy to imagine shadowy figures pulling the strings behind the scenes. The beauty of agency detection? It gives us a sense of control over the chaos.

Fear and uncertainty? They're like jet fuel for conspiracy theories. In times of crisis—say, a global pandemic—conspiracy theories emerge like wildfire. Why? Because fear demands answers. And these theories provide simple, digestible explanations for complex problems. They give us a sense of power over the unknown.

Let's not forget **group identity**. Conspiracy theories aren't just about beliefs—they're about belonging. When you join a community of like-minded truth-seekers, there's validation, a sense of purpose. That's why leaving these beliefs behind can feel like leaving a family. The emotional bond is often stronger than any piece of contradictory evidence.

And let's be honest—**distrust in authority** plays a massive role. We've been lied to before, right? From Watergate to the Tuskegee Syphilis Study, history is full of examples of governments and institutions hiding the truth. So, when someone says "they're lying to us," people are ready to listen. That's why alternative explanations—no matter how wild—can feel more credible than the official narrative. The more they've deceived us in the past, the harder it is to trust them now.

But it's not just about psychology; **personality traits** matter too. Those who are naturally skeptical, contrarian, or who crave uniqueness are more likely to embrace conspiracy theories. These individuals don't just want to fit in with the crowd—they want to stand out, to hold knowledge that others don't. Conspiracy theories offer them just that.

Finally, let's talk about the power of **media and misinformation**. Social media platforms? They're built to keep you engaged, and nothing grabs attention like controversy. Algorithms prioritize the content that gets the most clicks—often the most sensational or controversial. And let's be real, influencers and thought leaders know this. They wield enormous power, swaying opinions and giving credibility to these theories. It's a cycle that feeds itself—more clicks, more shares, more believers.

So, when we dig into why people believe conspiracy theories, it's not just a matter of being gullible. It's an intricate mix of cognitive biases, emotional needs, social connections, media influence, and years of betrayal and misinformation. Governments and powerful institutions have concealed truths for decades, fostering an environment of skepticism. Each scandal or cover-up only deepens public distrust, prompting individuals to seek alternative explanations for events that seem too orchestrated to be random. This persistent cycle of deception invites speculation and empowers the belief that unveiling hidden truths is essential to reclaiming agency in a world full of manipulation.

CHAPTER 2

THE CONSPIRACY THEORIST'S TOOLBOX

YOU'VE TAKEN YOUR FIRST steps into a deeper awareness, where curiosity and caution meet. The world you thought you knew? It might be more complex than it appears—shaped by forces with agendas that aren't always clear. But now that you're here, it's time to learn the tools of discernment.

This chapter is a toolkit, built to help you separate fact from fiction, signal from noise. Each technique and tool I'll introduce has been crafted through investigation and refined by study. Whether you're already well-versed in unraveling narratives or you're just starting out, these are the strategies to help you stay grounded, cut through distractions, and see things as they are. Take what resonates, use what works for you, and remember—this path is as much about questioning our perceptions as it is about what we discover. As you read, keep a balanced perspective: each tool is here to help you navigate complex information, but not every connection is intentional. Use your judgment and focus on what truly resonates.

Pattern Recognition: Seeing Through the Matrix

You think those "coincidences" plastered across the news are random? Think again. The ability to see hidden patterns is what separates the sheep from the wolves. It's time to sharpen your claws and identify the frameworks underlying complex events. One way to start is with **Timeline Mapping**, which exposes the choreographed chaos often underlying public events. This technique involves creating detailed timelines of supposedly "random" incidents, looking for recurring "coincidences" that smell of careful planning, familiar players who reappear under different guises, and policy changes that consistently benefit the powerful. Tools like Aeon Timeline or TimelineJS can help you visualize these connections, mapping out what looks like individual events but, in reality, forms a larger, orchestrated narrative. With these digital tools, you can practically see the "puppet strings" that connect disparate occurrences, revealing the structures behind the chaos.

Another useful technique is **Network Analysis**, which unmasks the complex webs that connect key players. This process involves mapping out the connections between influential individuals and organizations to reveal the hidden structures of power. Network analysis seeks out unexpected links between entities that may appear "unrelated" but actually work in tandem. It reveals people who keep showing up under different affiliations, along with organizations whose board members hold dual allegiances. Tools like Gephi and yEd are invaluable here; they act like x-ray machines, exposing the skeleton of these hidden networks and helping you lay bare the hidden framework of alliances and influence.

Deep Research: Digging Where They Don't Want You to Dig

Think the truth is handed to you on a silver platter? Wake up. It's buried under mountains of disinformation, a carefully constructed maze to hide what they don't want the public to know. To unearth this truth, you need **Deep Research**, which involves using advanced research techniques to dig beneath the surface of mainstream narratives. **Open Source Intelligence (OSINT) Gathering** is a powerful method within deep research, focusing on collecting information from publicly available sources. OSINT gathering often relies on using advanced search engine codes to track down information that has been deleted or concealed, resurrecting erased web pages with tools like the Wayback Machine—an internet archive that stores versions of websites long after they have been altered or removed.

Building a personal OSINT toolkit is like assembling a skeleton key for locked vaults of hidden information. It goes beyond bookmarks and becomes a collection of specialized resources that helps you navigate through oceans of data and uncover what "they" thought was hidden forever. Once you have gathered the initial data, **Cross-Referencing** becomes essential. Cross-referencing means checking every piece of intel from multiple sources and perspectives to ensure its accuracy. Rather than accepting the first "alternative" source you find, you should triangulate each claim, hunting down original documents like a bloodhound, since second-hand info is often unreliable. This technique allows you to look for cracks in the stories they propagate, as inconsistencies are where the light of truth often shines through. A tool like Hypothes.is can amplify this process by creating a collaborative environment for investigation, allowing a hive mind of truth-seekers to annotate and scrutinize information from every angle.

Symbolism Decryption: Reading Their Secret Language

They're talking right in front of you, but in a code designed to fly over the heads of the sleeping masses. It's time to break their cipher and understand **Symbolism Decryption**, the skill of reading between the lines of everyday messages. **Symbol Analysis** is the first step in this process. It involves decoding the meanings behind specific symbols that are carefully placed in media, architecture, logos, and public art. To master this, you need to develop what's often called a "third eye" for signs and symbols. The "language of the occult," or secret, esoteric symbolism, requires learning the deeper meanings behind shapes, colors, numbers, and other visual cues. As a starting point, *Dictionary of Symbols* by Chevalier and Gheerbrant isn't just a book—it's a comprehensive key to their hidden library, helping you start building a personal Rosetta Stone for understanding the hidden codes around you.

Going deeper into this hidden world involves techniques like **Steganography** and **Cryptography**, where hidden messages are embedded in plain sight. Steganography conceals data within other media, such as embedding a message within an image, while cryptography involves encoding messages in ciphers or symbols that need to be deciphered. Learning to spot patterns in supposedly random arrangements is key. With tools like Steghide and OpenStego, you can decode these messages, turning what seems like an ordinary photo or document into an encrypted story. These tools are your night-vision goggles, cutting through shadows to reveal the truth that's hidden within mundane images and texts.

Psy-Ops Detection: Shielding Your Mind from Their Invisible Weapons
Their most potent weapons aren't guns or bombs—they're aimed straight at your mind. **Psy-Ops (Psychological Operations) Detection** refers to understanding and countering covert tactics designed to influence public thought and behavior. The process of **Propaganda Analysis** is a crucial defense, helping you spot emotional manipulation embedded within the media. Propaganda is created using a set of classic techniques that play on our emotions and perceptions—methods that have been perfected over centuries to guide the masses. Understanding these techniques, such as fear appeals or bandwagon effects, gives you immunity from their influence. For example, keeping a "propaganda diary" where you log instances of manipulation will reveal patterns over time, helping you see through the fog of deceit.

Additionally, **Reverse Engineering Social Engineering** is a powerful skill that turns their weapons against them. Social engineering uses psychological manipulation to extract information or influence actions, often through verbal cues or **Neuro-Linguistic Programming (NLP)**—a psychological approach that shapes perceptions and emotions. By dissecting these speeches and analyzing their logical structures, you can recognize the subtle emotional triggers designed to bypass critical thinking. Practicing "de-spinning" news stories by stripping away emotional manipulation and logical fallacies allows you to see past the smoke and mirrors and catch a glimpse of the truth they're trying to hide.

Data Alchemy: Transforming Raw Information into Golden Truth

In this age of information warfare, the ability to process vast data streams is your secret weapon. **Data Alchemy** is the art of turning raw information into valuable insights, an essential skill in truth-seeking. **Data Mining** and **Web Scraping** are techniques that allow you to collect and extract data from large sources online, uncovering what they thought was safely buried. Data mining analyzes large datasets to detect hidden patterns, while web scraping collects data from websites. Starting with user-friendly tools like ParseHub or Octoparse helps you get your footing in gathering online data, but leveling up to custom scripts adds flexibility and precision.

Once data is collected, **Data Visualization** makes it easier to interpret. Data visualization transforms complex data into charts, graphs, and infographics, making hidden patterns visible and clear. Tools like Tableau and D3.js allow you to build visual representations that cut through disinformation, creating "truth bombs" that reveal the reality obscured by raw numbers. Creating "alternative visualizations" of official data can often reveal the real story, as a simple change in perspective exposes lies embedded in official numbers.

Secure Communications: Building an Underground Railroad of Truth

In a world where every word is monitored, protecting your sources—and yourself—isn't paranoia. It's survival. **Secure Communications** involves mastering the tools of anonymous and encrypted channels to shield your exchanges from prying eyes. **Digital Fortress Building** entails using secure messaging applications like Signal or Wire, which offer end-to-end encryption, ensuring that your messages vanish without a trace. For email encryption, PGP (Pretty Good Privacy) can encrypt content so that only the intended recipient can read it, turning your words into unbreakable code.

But when even digital communication becomes unsafe, **Analog Tradecraft** comes into play. Analog tradecraft, or secure offline info exchange, uses Cold War-style tactics such as physical "dead drops"—secret locations where messages or items are left for someone to collect later. Additionally, modern steganography can hide messages in mundane objects, such as a coded ad in a newspaper. Sometimes, the old methods are safest in a world where digital surveillance is rampant.

Psychological Fortification: Armoring Your Mind for the Truth War

The path of a truth-seeker is lonely and brutal. You need more than just knowledge—you need unbreakable mental armor. **Psychological Fortification** involves techniques to shield your mind from the stresses of relentless truth-seeking. **Cognitive Reframing** helps you build mental resilience by shifting how you process difficult truths, often using mindfulness as a tool to stay clear-headed. Practicing mindfulness is not about relaxing—it's about staying sharp, maintaining focus, and developing compartmentalization skills to separate your mission from daily life. Keeping a "Truth Journal" isn't just a diary; it's a record of your evolution as a human lie detector, a place to reflect on your insights and document your growth.

Equally crucial is building a truth tribe, a network of fellow awakened minds who support each other in the pursuit of truth. By finding allies in online forums and organizing local meet-ups, you can establish a trusted circle that becomes your personal truth special forces unit. Set protocols for vetting new members, as infiltrators are inevitable in any serious truth-seeking network. A truth tribe isn't just a group—it's your fortress in the war for the truth.

Predictive Analytics: Staying One Step Ahead of Their Game

Don't just react to their moves—anticipate them. It's time to start playing chess while they're still playing checkers. **Predictive Analytics** enables you to foresee actions and outcomes, leveraging historical patterns and data to anticipate future events. **Trend Forecasting** allows you to study past patterns, uncovering the long game of influential players from government agencies to secret societies. By identifying early warning signs of false flags or manufactured crises, you can start to see through time, mapping alternative futures and seeing possibilities that are often hidden.

The art of **War Gaming** is another crucial skill, borrowing military-style planning to stay one step ahead. By creating psychological profiles of key players and mapping out complex decision trees that outline possible moves and counter-moves, you can preemptively prepare for their next steps. Regular "war game" sessions with your truth cell allow you to simulate scenarios and hone your responses. With constant updates, you ensure your strategies evolve, so when their next false flag drops, you'll be ready.

The Never-Ending Battle for Truth

Remember this: the tools in this arsenal are just the beginning. The world of conspiracy—of hidden truths and massive deceptions—is ever-evolving. So too must your skills, your techniques, and your resolve.

This isn't a game. It's not some intellectual exercise. It's a war—a war for the future, for freedom, for the very nature of reality itself. They have the money, the power, the control of mass media. But we have something more powerful: the truth and the tools to find it. As you move through this book and beyond, come back to this chapter often. Sharpen your weapons. Upgrade your armor. Adapt to their tactics. The truth is out there, hidden in plain sight, obscured by a web of lies so vast most people live their entire lives without ever glimpsing it.

Now that you're equipped with the tools to decode misinformation and spot the tactics used to manipulate the mainstream narrative, you're ready to dive into what you came for: the theories themselves. The rest of this book is where the real action happens—where we dig into the hidden histories, government secrets, shadowy elites, and everything that's been kept just out of your reach. These are the stories they don't want you to believe or investigate. They want you stagnant, scrolling on your device, assuming everything they write is factual.

As you continue, keep in mind: truth-seeking is about staying open to discovery rather than jumping to conclusions. Remain grounded, use these tools wisely, and let your focus stay on evidence. Above all, remember to approach each technique rationally and thoughtfully—truth-seeking is about clarity, not paranoia. Get ready because the next chapters will take you deep into the labyrinth of deception and hidden truths. This is where the adventure begins.

CHAPTER 3

CLASSIC CONSPIRACIES THAT SHAPED THE WORLD

ON A SUNNY NOVEMBER day in 1963, President John F. Kennedy rode through Dallas, Texas, in an open-top convertible. The streets were packed with cheering crowds, a scene of optimism that quickly turned to horror. Shots rang out, and within moments, Kennedy lay mortally wounded. The assassination of JFK sent shockwaves across the globe and ignited one of the most enduring and controversial conspiracy theories in modern history.

The JFK Assassination: Unraveling the Mystery

In 1963, America was captivated by President John F. Kennedy, a leader who symbolized hope, progress, and a commitment to tackling urgent issues of the time—civil rights, space exploration, and Cold War diplomacy. He represented the potential for a stronger, more united America. But on November 22, that promise of leadership and forward momentum was violently cut short. As Kennedy's motorcade moved through Dealey Plaza in Dallas, Texas, three gunshots echoed through the crowd. President Kennedy was struck twice: a first bullet passing through his neck and a second, fatal shot hitting his head. Texas Governor John Connally, seated in front of him, was also injured. Rushed to Parkland Memorial Hospital, Kennedy was pronounced dead shortly after arrival, leaving the nation in shock and disbelief.

In the aftermath, President Lyndon B. Johnson established the Warren Commission to investigate the tragedy and provide an official narrative to the American people. After extensive examination, the Commission concluded that a lone gunman, Lee Harvey Oswald, was responsible for Kennedy's assassination. Oswald, a former U.S. Marine known for his Marxist sympathies and defection to the Soviet Union, reportedly acted independently. Positioned on the sixth floor of the Texas School Book Depository, Oswald is said to have fired three shots as the motorcade passed below.

A focal point of the Commission's findings was the "single-bullet theory." According to this theory, one bullet passed through Kennedy's neck before injuring Governor Connally in multiple locations. The report argued that the bullet's path was consistent with the motorcade's layout and the injuries both men sustained. Although this explanation has been essential to the official account, its acceptance has faced challenges from those who question the bullet's trajectory and the forensic evidence backing it.

Oswald's background was meticulously examined in the investigation. He was an enigmatic figure—trained as a marksman in the Marines, an ideologically complex individual with reported pro-Communist leanings, and a man who had once defected to the Soviet Union only to return to the United States. On the day of the assassination, Oswald was arrested at the Texas Theatre, where he had fled after allegedly killing Dallas police officer J.D. Tippit. He was detained on charges related to both deaths but would never stand trial. Two days after his arrest, nightclub owner Jack Ruby shot Oswald in the basement of the Dallas Police Headquarters. The killing, broadcast live on television, sealed Oswald's fate and effectively silenced the primary suspect.

Ruby's actions and Oswald's death left the Commission without a key witness. While Ruby claimed he acted out of grief for Kennedy, his ties to organized crime introduced more complexity into an already tangled case. Nonetheless, the Commission dismissed any notions of conspiracy, asserting that Oswald had acted alone, with no evidence of a broader plot or additional shooters involved.

The Warren Commission's report, encompassing nearly 900 pages, documented evidence from ballistics, eyewitness accounts, and Oswald's known associations, concluding that he alone bore responsibility for Kennedy's death. This official account, meticulously compiled, stands as the government's definitive statement on the events of that day, despite lingering questions and emerging theories.

Unveiling the Assassination Plot
For decades, the Warren Commission's report has stood as the government's official version of President John F. Kennedy's assassination: a lone gunman, Lee Harvey Oswald, acted alone, ending the life of a promising leader and altering the course of history. But as time passed, cracks in this story began to surface, and those cracks have grown into a full collapse. The evidence doesn't just suggest an alternative view—it screams that the American public was lied to, and that Kennedy's death was no random act, but a coldly calculated event with layers of deception.

Let's start with the single-bullet theory, the linchpin of the Warren Commission's find-ings. According to the report, a single bullet fired from Oswald's rifle managed to hit both Kennedy and Texas Governor John Connally, causing multiple wounds along a bizarre trajectory that defies logic. But forensic evidence, video footage from the Zapruder film, and analyses by experts over the years have exposed glaring inconsistencies. The bullet's path simply doesn't add up without the presence of another shooter. This single-bullet fantasy was designed to make the lone-gunman story plausible. In reality, it is anything but.

Then there's the undeniable acoustic evidence. An overlooked recording from a Dallas police officer's radio captured audio of four gunshots, not three, as the government insists. This extra shot points unmistakably to a second shooter—one that the official story conveniently omits. The 1970s House Select Committee on Assassinations even went so far as to conclude that a "probable conspiracy" was behind the assassination. Yet, despite this stunning admission, the identity of any additional shooters remains officially unknown.

Eyewitness testimonies paint an even grimmer picture of the day. Many bystanders reported hearing shots from multiple directions, especially from the infamous grassy knoll—a detail ignored by the Commission but impossible to dismiss. Some witnesses even saw figures lurking in that area, yet the government chose to bury these accounts. Why? Because acknowledging these witnesses would dismantle the entire lone-gunman story they were so desperate to sell.

To reinforce this point, consider the mysterious presence of the "Babushka Lady" in Dealey Plaza, a figure seen filming from a crucial vantage point at the time of the assassi-nation. Despite appearing in multiple photographs and videos, she was never identified, nor was her film footage ever located—an oversight that raises further questions about hidden evidence and the suppression of key testimonies. This figure, along with other overlooked eyewitnesses, highlights the deliberate choices in the investigation to ignore critical elements that would disrupt the official narrative.

So, let's say it was a lone gunman. If that were indeed the case, does the rest of the narrative line up? Well, Oswald himself, supposedly a skilled marksman, wasn't anything of the sort. His Marine records show him to be an average shooter, far from the expert sniper the official story claims. And yet we're told that he accomplished an extraordinary feat of marksmanship under extreme pressure. It's far more likely that the true assassins were hidden in plain sight and that Oswald was merely a convenient scapegoat.

The deception runs even deeper when we examine Jack Ruby's actions. Ruby—a man with close connections to organized crime—gunned down Oswald before he could even testify, supposedly out of sympathy for Kennedy's widow. But was that really Ruby's motive? Or was he eliminating Oswald to keep him silent? Ruby's convenient access to Oswald inside the Dallas Police Headquarters hints at something more sinister: a coordinated effort to make sure Oswald would never speak a word in court.

The CIA and FBI's roles in this cover-up are undeniable. Declassified documents reveal that both agencies had been watching Oswald long before the assassination and, even more shockingly, deliberately withheld crucial information from the Warren Commission. If Oswald was under surveillance, why weren't these details presented in the official investigation? Why the secrecy, unless they had something to hide?

In the years since Kennedy's death, more and more redacted documents have come to light, hinting at covert operations and cover-ups that go beyond Oswald or any single actor. This is the truth: the official story is a carefully constructed lie, crafted to shield powerful interests. As more evidence emerges, it becomes clear that Kennedy's death was a conspiracy, orchestrated and concealed by the very agencies meant to serve and protect the American people.

November 22, 1963, wasn't just an assassination. It was the beginning of a lie—one the government has spent decades defending. The reality is darker and far more complex than they ever wanted us to see. The time has come to look past the official narrative and see Kennedy's assassination for what it truly was: a ruthless elimination by forces threatened by a leader pushing against their agendas.

Kennedy's bold vision and resistance to entrenched power marked him as a target. His defiance of the status quo challenged plans set by powerful entities, who could not allow his influence to derail their objectives. The assassination wasn't just an isolated tragedy—it was a decisive move to silence a leader who threatened to reshape the system they controlled. Decades later, these powerful forces still work to keep the truth buried, unwilling to let their secrets see the light.

The Roswell UFO Incident: Fact or Fiction?

In the summer of 1947, rancher Mac Brazel stumbled upon a scattered field of strange debris on his property near Roswell, New Mexico. The fragments, which included rubber strips, tinfoil, and thick, paper-like material, didn't match anything Brazel had seen before. Confused and curious, he brought some of the debris to Sheriff George Wilcox, who then contacted officials at the nearby Roswell Army Air Field (RAAF) for further investigation. The military responded quickly, collecting the debris and making an initial, surprising statement to the public: they had recovered what they described as a "flying disc."

This announcement immediately grabbed national attention. The idea of a flying disc sparked the public's imagination, leading many to speculate about unidentified flying objects and extraterrestrial visitors. But just as quickly as the statement had been released, the military changed its narrative. Officials at RAAF retracted the claim, explaining that the debris was not a flying disc but rather the remains of a weather balloon. According to this revised statement, the initial description was simply a misunderstanding of the debris Brazel found.

With the weather balloon explanation, the incident was seemingly resolved, and public interest in the story faded. For many, the Roswell case was closed—an unusual find, misinterpreted as something more mysterious than it actually was. However, the story of Roswell would not stay buried. Decades later, in the 1990s, the U.S. Air Force released a new report that offered an updated official explanation. This report claimed that the debris Brazel found was not from an ordinary weather balloon but from "Project Mogul," a classified military project involving high-altitude balloons equipped with specialized sensors. Project Mogul's purpose was to detect sound waves from potential Soviet nuclear tests during the height of the Cold War, and secrecy around the project was essential to national security.

The government's revised story clarified that the initial flying disc announcement had been an error, quickly corrected to protect the secrecy of Project Mogul. The military explained that any tight-lipped responses to public inquiries were due to the classified nature of Cold War projects, not to conceal evidence of extraterrestrial life. With this new report, the official narrative reinforced that the Roswell incident was simply a matter of Cold War secrecy rather than a visitation from beyond Earth.

Today, the official stance on the Roswell incident remains that it was a misidentified military balloon project and nothing more. According to the government, the mystery at Roswell was resolved decades ago, a chapter of Cold War history closed as quickly as it began.

Secrets in the Nevada Desert

Area 51, hidden away in the Nevada desert, has been the government's best-kept secret for decades. Officially, it's just a military testing site, but this story barely scratches the surface. The fact is, Area 51 is shrouded in layers of lies. After years of outright denial, the government reluctantly acknowledged the base's existence in 2013, yet offered no transparency about what truly goes on there. And with decades of evidence stacking up, it's clear why: Area 51 isn't hiding military technology—it's hiding extraterrestrial technology, brought to Earth from beyond our world.

The government's official story crumbles under scrutiny. Area 51's proximity to Roswell is no coincidence. After the infamous 1947 crash, the weather balloon narrative was pushed to the public. But insiders have known all along that Roswell involved alien wreckage and, possibly, extraterrestrial bodies. That wreckage and those bodies were taken to Area 51, where scientists and military experts have spent decades studying them. Countless witnesses—former military personnel, employees, and even local residents—have reported seeing strange, otherworldly objects in the skies above Area 51. The sheer volume and consistency of these accounts cannot be dismissed as mere coincidence or misidentification.

One of the most compelling sources is Bob Lazar, a man who risked everything to expose the truth in 1989. Lazar claims to have worked at a highly classified facility near Area 51 known as S-4, where he saw and worked directly on alien spacecraft. He described intricate details: the propulsion systems, the antimatter reactors, and even the metallic structure of these crafts—technologies far beyond anything developed by humans. Lazar's story didn't just introduce new details; it unraveled the government's narrative. Attempts to discredit him, to erase his records, only underscore that Lazar was telling a truth the government desperately wanted to keep buried. If Area 51 was only a military testing ground, why the extreme lengths to silence him?

More evidence comes from the UFO sightings around Area 51, which have been relentless. For over half a century, witnesses have reported seeing strange lights and objects defying the laws of physics—silent, hovering, moving at speeds no aircraft could achieve, even today. The government's excuse? "Experimental aircraft." But these sightings continued long after the Cold War, when there would have been no need to test such prototypes in secret. Are we truly expected to believe that all these sightings, all these years, were just aircraft experiments? The evidence is too extensive, too consistent, to support this convenient dismissal.

Then there are the underground facilities, rumored to extend far beneath the desert surface, where it's said that alien technology, and perhaps even extraterrestrial life, are stored and studied. These facilities aren't just rumors; they are documented by former employees, by satellite imagery, and by those brave enough to speak out. What are they hiding beneath Area 51 if not the alien wreckage from Roswell and potentially live beings? The level of secrecy here goes beyond anything required for conventional military projects.

But it doesn't stop at technology and research. Some sources go as far as to suggest a covert agreement between the U.S. government and extraterrestrial entities—a pact allowing aliens to operate on Earth in exchange for access to advanced technology. This theory, outrageous as it sounds, explains the government's desperation to keep Area 51 locked down. Restricted airspace, surveillance at every corner, armed patrols authorized to use deadly force—if this were just a testing site, such extreme measures wouldn't be necessary. The government has created a fortress around Area 51 to protect something far more extraordinary than aircraft.

Recent years have seen the government carefully release limited information on UFOs, showcasing pilot footage and brief reports. But these disclosures are designed to pacify the public without exposing the deeper truth. Each "disclosure" is tightly controlled, avoiding any mention of what's really happening at Area 51. The message is clear: they're throwing the public breadcrumbs, hoping we won't ask for the whole story.

The truth is right in front of us: Area 51 is not some simple military base. It is a vault of secrets, a site dedicated to studying, storing, and potentially replicating alien technology. The security, the secrecy, the selective "disclosures" all point to one undeniable fact—Area 51 is hiding something extraordinary, something the government believes we cannot handle. How much longer can they keep the lid on this monumental cover-up? The facts are there for those willing to see, and it's time we demand the truth.

The Illuminati: Myth or Reality?

In 1776, Adam Weishaupt, a professor of canon law at the University of Ingolstadt in Bavaria, founded the Bavarian Illuminati. His vision was to establish a society that would champion the ideals of the Enlightenment—reason, science, secularism, and individual freedom—in a world largely dominated by religious and monarchical authorities. The Illuminati sought to foster a society governed by rational thought and intellectual advancement rather than tradition or superstition. Members were carefully selected for their commitment to these ideals, and strict secrecy was required to protect the group's activities. Operating in small, autonomous cells, members maintained anonymity, a method designed to prevent infiltration and ensure loyalty.

The Illuminati's members included intellectuals, political figures, and writers, all of whom shared Weishaupt's vision of social reform and progressive governance. Weishaupt aimed for the group to subtly influence political decisions and societal norms, but he envisioned achieving these goals through enlightenment rather than open opposition to existing structures. However, the Illuminati's growth and its secretive methods eventually attracted the attention of the Bavarian government. Concerned about the group's influence and potential impact on the established order, the Bavarian government banned all secret societies in 1785, specifically targeting the Illuminati. Weishaupt fled Bavaria, and the organization was officially disbanded.

Although the Bavarian Illuminati had a relatively brief existence, its secretive nature and ambitious goals captured the public's imagination. Over the years, rumors began to circulate about the group's continued existence, with theories suggesting that the Illuminati had simply gone underground and continued to operate discreetly, influencing global events from behind the scenes.

In modern times, the Illuminati has evolved into a powerful symbol within conspiracy theories. Theories about a "new" Illuminati describe it as a secret society with far-reaching influence over global politics, finance, and media. According to these theories, this modern Illuminati comprises influential families and figures, often associated with elite political and financial institutions. Families such as the Rothschilds and the Rockefellers are frequently mentioned as central members, allegedly manipulating global markets and political systems to consolidate power. Symbols like the Eye of Providence and the pyramid are commonly linked to the Illuminati and are claimed to be hidden in corporate logos, currency, and various forms of media, supposedly as subtle signals of the group's pervasive influence.

Historically, however, there is no verified evidence to support the idea of a modern-day Illuminati or its control over world events. Scholars and historians agree that while the original Bavarian Illuminati existed briefly, there is no conclusive proof that the organization survived or that it evolved into the kind of global entity described in conspiracy theories. Claims of hidden symbols, alleged insider testimonies, and circumstantial links are often explained as coincidences, creative decisions, or the result of misinterpretation rather than evidence of an organized secret society. "Experts" maintain that the modern concept of the Illuminati is largely a myth, shaped by cultural fears of hidden power structures rather than rooted in historical fact.

Despite this, Illuminati theories have had a significant impact on popular culture and society. The idea of a hidden elite influencing global events appeals to those who feel distrustful of established power structures, particularly in an age of rapid social and technological change. Online platforms such as YouTube, Reddit, and Facebook have enabled the rapid spread of Illuminati theories, making them accessible to a wide audience and fostering communities where these ideas are continually discussed and reinforced.

Accusations of Illuminati involvement have even extended to celebrities and high-profile figures. Musicians, actors, and political leaders are frequently linked to the Illuminati based on symbolic interpretations or perceived associations. Figures like Beyoncé, Jay-Z, and political leaders such as Barack Obama are commonly targeted, usually without concrete evidence, but their inclusion in these theories adds intrigue to the narrative and keeps the concept of a modern Illuminati alive in the public imagination.

Unveiling the Truth Behind the Illuminati
The line between myth and reality regarding the Illuminati has been deliberately blurred, keeping the public unaware of a darker, more complex reality: a powerful network with a calculated agenda to establish a New World Order through manipulation and control. While the Bavarian Illuminati is often portrayed as a short-lived Enlightenment group, the truth of its influence and persistence goes much deeper—and it didn't end in the 18th century.

From its inception, the Illuminati's ambitions extended far beyond promoting reason and free thought. The group sought to infiltrate and dismantle existing power structures—religious and monarchical authorities—through covert means, reshaping society from the shadows. Operating under the guise of intellectual discourse, the Illuminati's true aim reached into politics, economics, and social control. This secretive structure, with members working in isolated cells, allowed the group to operate largely invisibly while exerting influence on critical events of their time and beyond.

The official story that the Illuminati disbanded after the Bavarian government's crackdown in 1785 is misleading. Instead, the Illuminati went underground, continuing to operate behind the scenes and evolving into a far more powerful force. Rather than being dismantled, the Illuminati expanded its reach globally, infiltrating key governments, financial institutions, and religious organizations—all in pursuit of a New World Order.

The claim that the Illuminati's influence was limited to Bavaria is a convenient myth. Evidence points to the Illuminati's role in igniting the French Revolution, orchestrating the overthrow of monarchies, and spreading revolutionary ideals across Europe. Covert meetings and correspondence between revolutionary leaders and secret societies clearly point to the Illuminati's early influence in radical shifts that changed the course of history.

Today, the Illuminati's reach extends globally, quietly controlling world events. The symbols often associated with the Illuminati—such as the all-seeing eye and the pyramid—are not random designs but deliberate symbols, signaling allegiance to this hidden order. These symbols appear on global currency, government seals, and popular media, subtly reminding those in the know of the power held by those loyal to the Illuminati's mission.

Credible whistleblowers have revealed the Illuminati's influence in shaping global politics, economics, and culture. Figures like John Robison and Augustin Barruel in the 19th century uncovered links between the Illuminati and various political movements, including socialism, communism, and later capitalist elites. Their revelations provide a foundation for the theory that the Illuminati controls a hidden network of global elites.

Declassified government records, such as those from the FBI and CIA, which claim to "debunk" Illuminati involvement, appear to be part of a larger cover-up. Intelligence agencies often act in the interests of those in power—many of whom are directly connected to the Illuminati's goals. Far from providing clarity, these declassified reports only reinforce the view that the Illuminati's influence has been hidden from official records to maintain its secrecy.

The media and entertainment industries, controlled by this same shadowy elite, play a critical role in perpetuating the Illuminati's control. High-profile figures in music, film, and politics publicly display Illuminati symbols as markers of allegiance to this hidden order. This isn't mere speculation; the consistent use of these symbols across platforms suggests an orchestrated effort to normalize and obscure the true nature of the Illuminati's influence.

The Illuminati has never ceased to exist. Instead, it has evolved into a vast network of secret societies and global elites who manipulate the world's financial systems, governments, and social movements to their advantage. Their ultimate goal? The establishment of a New World Order—a centralized global government in which the Illuminati holds absolute control, leaving the rest of humanity in darkness.

The persistence of the Illuminati "myth" is not merely a result of overactive imaginations; it's a reflection of a deeper reality. As we examine further conspiracies in this book, the extent of these organizations' control over the world becomes undeniable. From media manipulation to hidden influence in politics, the Illuminati's reach extends far beyond what most dare to believe.

In conclusion, while the historical Illuminati may have started in Bavaria, its ongoing influence is far more sinister. With their hands in nearly every aspect of global governance, the Illuminati remains a powerful, secretive force shaping our world today. As we continue to uncover government secrets and cover-ups, the question remains: How much control have they already gained, and what is their next move?

CHAPTER 4

GOVERNMENT SECRETS AND COVER-UPS

IN THE EARLY 1960S, a series of covert plans emerged from the depths of the Pentagon that seemed straight out of a spy novel. These plans, collectively known as Operation Northwoods, proposed shocking measures to manipulate public opinion and justify military action against Cuba. As you explore the details of this audacious scheme, you'll uncover the lengths governments might go to achieve their objectives, sometimes at the expense of truth and morality.

Operation Northwoods: A Government Deception

To understand Operation Northwoods, you must first consider the historical context from which it emerged. The Cold War tensions between the United States and Cuba were at an all-time high during the early 1960s. Fidel Castro had recently overthrown the American-backed dictator Fulgencio Batista, establishing a communist regime that aligned closely with the Soviet Union. This shift posed a significant threat to U.S. interests in the Western Hemisphere. The fear of communist expansion was palpable, and American policymakers were desperate to contain it.

The Bay of Pigs invasion in April 1961, a CIA-backed attempt to overthrow Castro using Cuban exiles, had ended in a catastrophic failure. The operation was poorly executed and met with fierce resistance from Castro's forces, resulting in the capture or death of most of the invaders. The failure of the Bay of Pigs not only embarrassed the Kennedy administration but also heightened the urgency to find alternative means to remove Castro from power. In this climate of desperation and fear, the Joint Chiefs of Staff conceived Operation Northwoods.

Operation Northwoods was a series of proposals that aimed to create a pretext for military intervention in Cuba. The plans included a variety of false-flag operations designed to deceive the American public and the international community into supporting an invasion. One of the most startling proposals involved staging attacks on American soil and blaming them on the Cuban government. These fabricated attacks included the idea of hijacking planes and bombing U.S. cities. The planners even suggested using fake casualties and staged funerals to add realism to their deception. The goal was to incite public outrage and generate support for a military response against Cuba.

The ethical and political implications of Operation Northwoods are staggering. The plan involved deliberately deceiving the American public, a violation of the trust between the government and its citizens. The use of false-flag attacks would have not only manipulated public opinion but also potentially resulted in real harm to innocent people. Internationally, the fallout could have been severe. Accusing Cuba of unprovoked aggression based on fabricated evidence would have further strained U.S.-Cuba relations. It could have escalated tensions with the Soviet Union, risking a broader conflict during a period already fraught with nuclear threats.

Internally, Operation Northwoods was met with opposition and debate. President Kennedy ultimately rejected the plan, recognizing its moral and political dangers. However, the fact that such a proposal was seriously considered highlights the extreme measures some officials were willing to take to achieve their objectives. The ethical concerns about deceiving the public and the potential for international fallout underscore Cold War-era policymaking's complex and often dark nature.

The details of Operation Northwoods remained classified for decades, hidden from public scrutiny. It wasn't until the 1990s, when documents were declassified that the full extent of the plan came to light. The revelations sparked outrage and disbelief among the public. Many struggled to comprehend that their government had seriously contemplated such deceptive and dangerous actions. The declassification of these documents provided a rare glimpse into the inner workings of Cold War strategy and the lengths to which officials were willing to go to counter perceived threats.

The public reaction to the revelations was one of shock and betrayal. Operation Northwoods became a symbol of government overreach and the potential for abuse of power. It reinforced the skepticism many Americans felt towards their government, particularly in the wake of other scandals and cover-ups that came to light during the same period. The impact on public trust was profound, contributing to a growing disillusionment with political institutions.

The legacy of Operation Northwoods continues to resonate today. It serves as a caution-ary tale about the dangers of unchecked power and the importance of transparency and accountability in government. Examining this dark chapter in history gives you a deeper understanding of the ethical complexities and moral dilemmas that can arise in pursuing national security. The story of Operation Northwoods challenges you to question the narratives presented by those in power and to remain vigilant against the potential for deception and manipulation.

The Broader Implications for Government Accountability

Operation Northwoods is a striking example of the potential for government overreach, revealing the darker side of policymaking when national security is used to justify extreme measures. The very nature of this proposal raises serious questions about the balance of power and the ethical responsibilities of those in leadership. When a government is willing to deceive its own citizens and manipulate public opinion to pursue its goals, it undermines the foundations of trust and transparency upon which democratic systems rely.

The concept of government accountability becomes critical when exploring cases like Operation Northwoods. It demonstrates how secrecy and the pursuit of control can lead to proposals disregarding ethical boundaries, putting innocent lives at risk for strategic gain. This pattern of behavior, where clandestine actions are considered or even executed behind closed doors, reveals the fragility of public trust and the dangers posed when power is unchecked.

Moreover, the revelation of these covert plans, often years or decades after they were conceived, reinforces the importance of transparency in government. When classified information comes to light, it can shock and disturb the public, prompting feelings of betrayal and disillusionment. This erosion of trust doesn't simply fade—it lingers, casting a shadow over future decisions and actions taken by those in power.

Operation Northwoods is a cautionary tale about the lengths governments may go to pursue their objectives. It challenges us to reflect on the broader implications of unchecked authority, raising critical questions about ensuring that ethical principles are upheld, even in the face of national security concerns. In examining these patterns of deception and manipulation, we are reminded of the essential role of accountability, transparency, and vigilance in safeguarding democratic values.

Watergate: The Deep Throat Revelation

On June 17, 1972, five men were arrested for breaking into the Democratic National Committee headquarters in the Watergate complex, Washington, D.C. The men, later linked to the Committee to Re-Elect the President (CRP) for President Nixon, were discovered to be attempting to wiretap phones and steal confidential documents. This break-in, initially appearing as a minor burglary, soon unraveled into a massive political scandal when links were traced back to members of Nixon's administration and re-election committee, revealing a systematic abuse of power.

The Nixon administration quickly attempted to distance itself from the break-in and covered up its connections by obstructing the FBI's investigation, using CIA pressure, paying "hush money" to the burglars, and creating false narratives to deflect blame. Despite these efforts, investigative journalists Bob Woodward and Carl Bernstein from *The Washington Post*, assisted by information from a key anonymous source known only as "Deep Throat" (later identified as FBI Deputy Director Mark Felt), persistently reported on the case. Their reporting exposed connections between the Nixon administration, the CRP, and a broader pattern of political espionage against perceived "enemies."

Following the media revelations, the U.S. Senate initiated hearings in early 1973, led by the Senate Watergate Committee, and public hearings were broadcast nationwide, drawing public scrutiny. A key moment in the hearings came with the testimony of former White House counsel John Dean, who accused Nixon of direct involvement in the cover-up. Additionally, it was revealed that Nixon had a secret taping system in the White House that recorded conversations. When special prosecutor Archibald Cox demanded these tapes, Nixon initially refused, sparking a constitutional crisis known as the "Saturday Night Massacre," in which Nixon ordered the firing of Cox. This led to the resignation of several top Justice Department officials and further intensified public backlash.

The tapes eventually were released, although some sections were mysteriously missing, and they contained evidence implicating Nixon in the cover-up, particularly in discussions of obstructing the FBI's investigation. Facing mounting evidence and near-certain impeachment, Nixon announced his resignation on August 8, 1974, making him the first U.S. president to resign from office. Vice President Gerald Ford then assumed the presidency and later issued Nixon a controversial pardon, preventing him from facing potential criminal charges.

In the scandal's aftermath, significant reforms were enacted to prevent similar abuses of executive power. The Ethics in Government Act of 1978 imposed restrictions on campaign finance and created the Federal Election Commission (FEC) to enforce campaign finance laws. Public trust in the government was deeply shaken, leading to a shift in American political culture marked by skepticism toward political leaders. The Watergate scandal highlighted the critical role of investigative journalism and reinforced the importance of checks and balances within U.S. democracy.

The official narrative stands that Watergate was a profound breach of public trust, exposing the lengths to which Nixon's administration went to retain power through illegal means, including obstruction of justice, abuse of power, and manipulation of federal agencies. This narrative emphasizes the resilience of U.S. democratic institutions in holding even the highest offices accountable.

The Political Targeting Behind Watergate

The official story of Watergate paints it as a straightforward abuse of power by the Nixon administration. However, digging deeper reveals a more complex and politically charged narrative. Rather than merely a case of corruption and cover-up, some argue Watergate was an orchestrated effort to remove President Nixon for political reasons—much like how Donald Trump is being targeted through the court system today. Far from being a mere scandal, Watergate may have been a premeditated move by powerful forces within Washington, working behind the scenes to discredit Nixon and dismantle his presidency.

One prevailing theory is that Nixon was intentionally framed and set up by political adversaries determined to bring him down. Those who support this view suggest that factions within the intelligence community—particularly the FBI and CIA—had their own motivations to see Nixon's downfall, especially as he worked to reduce their influence and power. Nixon's foreign policy moves, including détente with the Soviet Union and opening relations with China, upset the established order, prompting these intelligence agencies to act against him. Watergate, in this light, was less about a burglary and more about orchestrating a crisis that could be used to push Nixon out of office.

The involvement of FBI Deputy Director Mark Felt, better known as Deep Throat, plays a critical role in this theory. While Felt's leaks to the media have been portrayed as acts of integrity, some believe they were driven by personal ambition and political motives. Felt was passed over for the position of FBI Director, and some argue his decision to leak was rooted in a desire for revenge rather than any noble pursuit of justice. His actions conveniently fueled the media firestorm that led to Nixon's resignation, raising questions about whether this was part of a larger political maneuver.

Moreover, the role of the media in escalating the Watergate crisis has come under scrutiny. While Woodward and Bernstein are celebrated for their investigative journalism, critics argue that the media's relentless focus on Nixon and the scandal was politically motivated. Certain journalists and outlets, aligned with anti-Nixon political factions, may have strategically amplified the scandal to weaken his presidency. This was not just about uncovering corruption but using the scandal to ensure Nixon's downfall—whether or not the full story of Watergate was as damning as portrayed.

Even the nature of the Watergate break-in itself raises suspicions. There are theories that Nixon may not have been directly involved in the planning of the break-in at all. Instead, rogue elements within his campaign or even within intelligence agencies could have acted independently, knowing the fallout would be pinned on Nixon. His later attempts to cover it up, then, might have been more about saving face and avoiding embarrassment rather than hiding direct involvement. Nixon's reaction could have been spun as guilt by those who wanted to exploit the situation for political gain.

Nixon's domestic and foreign policies had made him enemies on all sides, and these enemies saw Watergate as their opportunity to strike. His controversial stance on the Vietnam War, his drive for peace with China, and his steps to curb the power of the intelligence agencies all made him a prime target for removal. Watergate, seen through this lens, was the perfect tool—engineered to take down a president who threatened the existing power structures in Washington.

The aftermath of Watergate, including reforms like the establishment of the Federal Election Commission, has often been cited as necessary steps to curb executive power. But even these reforms have been viewed by some as part of the broader political targeting of Nixon—designed to ensure that future presidents would be constrained by new political mechanisms. Watergate was not just a scandal but a turning point, a carefully calculated political move that forever changed the balance of power in the U.S. government.

In drawing parallels to today, it's easy to see similarities in how political opponents are using legal and media systems to target Donald Trump. Just as Nixon was framed as the ultimate villain, some argue that Trump is being dragged through courtrooms in a similar bid to discredit him and prevent his return to power. Both men, disruptive in their politics and willing to challenge entrenched institutions, faced intense scrutiny and were pursued by powerful forces looking to remove them from the political stage.

Putting it all together, Watergate wasn't merely an isolated scandal about a break-in—it was an intentional political coup executed by intelligence factions within the government. The evidence points to a calculated effort by the CIA and FBI to dismantle Nixon's presidency. Bob Woodward, portrayed as an investigative journalist, was in fact a former Naval intelligence officer strategically placed at The Washington Post, working with high-ranking FBI officials to publicly dismantle Nixon's image and power.

Watergate serves as a warning: entrenched powers will employ any means necessary to protect their agendas, eliminating even the highest officeholder when it suits their interests. This was not justice—it was a high-stakes, covert takedown. As we explore further in this book, the story of Nixon's downfall is a reminder that political power plays are rarely as simple as they appear on the surface.

MKUltra: The CIA's Mind Control Program

The origins of MKUltra are deeply rooted in the post-World War II era, a time when fears of Soviet advancements in psychological and mind control techniques gripped the United States. The Cold War created an atmosphere of intense rivalry, with both superpowers seeking to gain any possible advantage. The CIA, concerned that the Soviets might develop methods to control human behavior, initiated MKUltra to explore the potential of mind control for interrogation and espionage. The goal was to develop techniques that could be used to manipulate individuals, extract information, and potentially create undetectable agents.

MKUltra's experiments were diverse and often disturbing. The program's most infamous method involved the administration of LSD and other psychoactive drugs to unwitting subjects. The CIA believed that these substances could be used to break down mental resistance and induce a state of suggestibility. Subjects, including military personnel, college students, and even ordinary citizens, were often dosed without their knowledge or consent. This led to unpredictable and sometimes tragic outcomes, as the effects of these drugs were not fully understood. In addition to drugs, MKUltra employed hypnosis and sensory deprivation techniques. Hypnosis was used to try to implant false memories or erase existing ones, while sensory deprivation aimed to break down an individual's sense of reality. Subjects were placed in isolation tanks or deprived of sensory input for extended periods, leading to severe psychological distress. The program also targeted vulnerable populations, such as prisoners and mental health patients, who were subjected to these experiments without proper oversight or ethical considerations.

The ethical and legal issues surrounding MKUltra are staggering. One of the most significant concerns is the subjects' lack of informed consent. People were often subjected to experimentation without their knowledge, violating their autonomy and dignity. This disregard for ethical standards resulted in numerous cases of psychological and physical harm. Many subjects experienced long-term trauma, and some even lost their lives due to the program's reckless practices. Congressional hearings in the 1970s, led by the Church Committee, brought some of MKUltra's abuses to light. The committee's investigations revealed the extent of the CIA's unethical behavior and led to calls for greater oversight and accountability. The hearings exposed the program's disregard for human rights and the rule of law, prompting public outrage and demands for reform.

The long-term impact of MKUltra on public perception and policy is profound. The program's declassification and public revelation in the 1970s shattered trust in intelligence agencies. The public learned that the CIA had conducted experiments on American citizens without their consent, leading to a widespread sense of betrayal. This erosion of trust has had lasting effects, contributing to ongoing skepticism about government transparency and accountability. MKUltra has also left an indelible mark on popular culture. Movies, TV shows, and literature have explored themes of mind control, often drawing inspiration from the program's real-life horrors. Films like "The Manchurian Candidate" and series like "Stranger Things" have captivated audiences with stories of government experiments and psychic powers, reflecting the enduring fascination with MKUltra's dark legacy. These cultural representations keep the memory of MKUltra alive, serving as a reminder of the potential dangers of unchecked power and secrecy.

Unveiling the Manson Connection
While the official accounts of MKUltra expose a chilling government program of secret mind control experiments, the true scope of its operations may be far more sinister than anyone has dared to admit. One of the most compelling theories, kept in the shadows of public discourse, is the connection between MKUltra and Charles Manson—a figure who, far from being just a deranged cult leader, may have been a pawn in a covert CIA experiment. Evidence suggests that the grisly Manson Family murders in 1969 could have been part of a broader, orchestrated government plot to manipulate society through mind control, with Manson playing his role as a test subject or even an asset.

Central to this theory is the prolific use of LSD—both in the MKUltra program and by Manson himself. The CIA's involvement in experimenting with LSD as a tool for mind control is well-documented, and Manson's own use of the drug to control and manipulate his followers is too striking to be mere coincidence. It is easy to see that the CIA could have supplied Manson with LSD, not only to experiment on him but to test the limits of psychological manipulation on a vulnerable, cult-like group. How else could Manson have obtained such quantities of the drug, and how else could he have maintained such an iron grip over his followers, who were willing to kill on command?

Manson's suspicious legal history fuels further intrigue. Despite repeatedly violating parole and accumulating a string of arrests, Manson appeared to enjoy an unusual level of protection and leniency from law enforcement. I argue this wasn't just a bureaucratic oversight—it was part of a larger, darker plan. That Manson was kept free and operational to serve as an ongoing subject for the CIA's study into mind control. I'll go further and suggest that allowing Manson to continue his operation was not only intentional but *necessary* for the government's covert social experiments. The lack of severe legal consequences, despite his criminal behavior, raises plenty of red flags about who was really pulling the strings behind the scenes.

Moreover, Manson's rise to infamy didn't just come out of nowhere—it aligned perfectly with the counterculture movement of the 1960s. It's easily arguable that the Manson Family murders were part of a CIA strategy to discredit the growing counterculture movement, which had embraced psychedelic drugs like LSD and stood against the establishment. By associating the brutal violence of the Manson Family with the peace-loving ethos of the hippie movement, the government could shift public opinion against those challenging the status quo. In this light, Manson wasn't simply a criminal mastermind but a tool—either knowingly or unknowingly—used to stoke fear and chaos, discrediting the very movements that threatened the government's control.

Though no *official* documents have yet surfaced explicitly linking Manson to MKUltra, the circumstantial evidence is enough to keep me convinced. Manson's access to drugs, his legal impunity, and his use of mind control techniques fit too closely with the known objectives of MKUltra to ignore. The fact that no concrete proof has been revealed only deepens the mystery and reminds us how far the government has gone to cover up such explosive stories.

The Manson case represents just the tip of the iceberg when it comes to MKUltra's reach. If Manson was, indeed, a product of government experimentation, it calls into question just how far the CIA went in its pursuit of psychological control. Was the Manson Family massacre simply a tragic outcome of one man's deranged leadership, or was it a planned social experiment meant to discredit the very movement that sought peace and freedom?

These questions challenge us to reconsider everything we think we know about the government's role in society. MKUltra has already shown us that the U.S. government had no qualms about experimenting on its own citizens, and the Manson connection, whether proven or not, taps into a deeper fear: that those in power are willing to manipulate even the darkest corners of human behavior to achieve their ends.

As you reflect on MKUltra, consider the profound ethical implications and the human cost of such experiments. Whether you focus on the confirmed abuses or the speculative connections like the Manson case, the program's legacy serves as a stark reminder of the critical need for oversight in government and scientific research. MKUltra challenges us to confront the moral boundaries of how far institutions should go in the pursuit of knowledge, power, and national security. As we move forward, the next chapter will dive deeper into other covert operations and secret projects, continuing to reveal the hidden layers of government actions and their lasting impact.

In the shadows of these historical events—whether verified or fueled by plausible theories—ethical dilemmas, power struggles, and the quest for control come to light. These stories compel all Americans to stay vigilant, questioning the narratives we are given and remaining mindful of the complex forces at play behind the scenes. As the exploration of government secrets continues, new insights will emerge, pushing us to reevaluate our understanding of authority, accountability, and our world.

CHAPTER 5

MODERN CONSPIRACIES IN THE SPOTLIGHT

ON A CLEAR SEPTEMBER morning in 2001, the world watched in shock as two commercial airliners crashed into the Twin Towers of the World Trade Center in New York City. Within hours, both towers collapsed, and another plane hit the Pentagon in Arlington, Virginia. A fourth plane, United Airlines Flight 93, crashed into a field in Pennsylvania after passengers attempted to overpower the hijackers. These coordinated attacks, carried out by 19 terrorists, forever changed the global landscape and ignited a wave of conspiracy theories that persist to this day.

9/11: Inside Job or Terrorist Attack?

The official narrative of the 9/11 attacks, as presented in the 9/11 Commission Report, outlines a series of coordinated terrorist events carried out by 19 hijackers linked to Al-Qaeda. The attack began at 8:46 AM on September 11, 2001, when American Airlines Flight 11 struck the North Tower of the World Trade Center. Seventeen minutes later, United Airlines Flight 175 hit the South Tower, and within hours, both towers collapsed due to the intense fires and structural damage.

Simultaneously, at 9:37 AM, American Airlines Flight 77 crashed into the Pentagon in Arlington, Virginia, causing significant casualties and damage. The fourth hijacked plane, United Airlines Flight 93, was likely headed for another target in Washington, D.C., but crashed in a Pennsylvania field after passengers fought to regain control, thwarting the attackers' plans.

According to the official account, the attacks were meticulously planned and orchestrated by Al-Qaeda, with a goal of inflicting maximum destruction and terror on the United States. This resulted in a seismic shift in U.S. policy and global security, launching the War on Terror and marking the beginning of military action in Afghanistan under Operation Enduring Freedom.

The Commission's report highlights intelligence gaps and coordination issues that allowed the attackers to proceed with their plan undetected, leading to calls for reforms across intelligence and aviation security. The legacy of 9/11, as framed by the official narrative, continues to shape both national security and public perceptions, emphasizing the need for vigilance against terrorism and resilience in the face of threats.

The Myriad of Conspiracies Behind 9/11

The official story of the September 11th attacks is a carefully crafted narrative that conceals the real forces at work. Far from being a spontaneous act of terror, the events of 9/11 were an "inside job" designed to justify military interventions, expand government control, and erode civil liberties. The 9/11 Truth Movement has uncovered compelling evidence that directly challenges the official narrative and reveals a web of lies, manipulation, and calculated deceit orchestrated by those in power. Since it is difficult to weave all the possibilities into one concrete statement, I will summarize the myriad of potential 9/11 alternatives to the official narrative. This is by no means an exhaustive list.

The Controlled Demolition Theory

The collapse of the Twin Towers was not the result of plane impacts or fire damage but a premeditated controlled demolition using explosives placed within the buildings. The near-perfect, symmetrical collapse of both towers, as well as their free-fall speed, is irrefutable evidence that the destruction was too precise to be accidental. This isn't just speculation—it's supported by structural engineers, architects, and demolition experts who have scientifically demonstrated that such a collapse could not have occurred without the deliberate use of explosives. The official explanation of structural failure falls apart when examining videos that clearly show "squibs"—small explosions below the impact zones—proving that timed detonations brought the towers down.

Despite the attempts of official investigations, such as those by NIST, to debunk this theory, the scientific evidence remains unchallenged. In fact, these investigations have been criticized for their failure to address or explain the key aspects of the towers' collapse, especially the speed and symmetry, which align with the characteristics of a controlled demolition. No matter how many reports are issued, they have not and cannot disprove what is scientifically evident: this was a planned demolition.

World Trade Center Building 7 (WTC 7) provides even more damning proof. WTC 7 collapsed later in the day without being hit by a plane, and yet it fell in a controlled manner, just like the towers. This building's mysterious collapse cannot be explained by fire or debris, as claimed by the official narrative. The only logical conclusion is that WTC 7 was brought down by a controlled demolition, further exposing the depth of the conspiracy. Once again, no investigation has adequately addressed or refuted the scientific evidence that supports this conclusion.

Additional evidence supporting a controlled demolition comes from accounts that officials told people evacuating the building to return to their offices, reflecting confidence in the towers' structural resilience. The World Trade Center towers were specifically engineered to withstand significant impacts, including an airplane collision, without collapsing. The complete failure of these structures from the impacts alone contradicts these engineering standards, suggesting that additional measures, such as explosives, were involved in bringing the towers down.

The "Stand Down" Theory

The failure of the U.S. military to intercept the hijacked planes on 9/11 was not a result of confusion or incompetence; it was a deliberate "stand down" ordered by key figures within the government. This was a calculated decision to allow the attacks to proceed in order to create a pretext for war. The delayed response, the deviation from standard protocols, and the suspicious actions of high-ranking officials all point to a government that knowingly let the attacks happen to advance a political agenda.

The aftermath of 9/11, with the wars in Afghanistan and Iraq and the implementation of the Patriot Act, confirms that this was all part of a broader strategy. The attacks were used to justify a massive military expansion and a drastic increase in government surveillance and control, giving the U.S. government unprecedented power over its citizens and the global stage.

Insider Trading and Financial Foreknowledge

The evidence of financial foreknowledge is yet another piece of this dark puzzle. In the days leading up to 9/11, there was an unusual spike in trading activity on United Airlines and American Airlines stocks. The sudden surge in "put options" indicates that certain individuals knew the attacks were coming and sought to profit from the devastation. The official investigation by the SEC claimed no connection to insider knowledge, but this is just another example of the government covering up the truth. The reality is that high-level insiders were aware of the impending attacks and took advantage of the opportunity to enrich themselves.

Flight 93: The Shootdown Theory

The official narrative of Flight 93, which claims that passengers heroically overpowered the hijackers, is a fabrication. The scattered debris and lack of significant wreckage indicate that the plane was shot down by the U.S. military to prevent it from reaching its target. The government's insistence that no military action was taken, combined with altered elements of the crash site story, points to a deliberate cover-up of the truth. Flight 93 was not brought down by passengers—it was destroyed mid-air by military intervention, a fact hidden to protect the government's role in this operation.

A Legacy of Mistrust and Suppression

The 9/11 Truth Movement exposes the uncomfortable reality that the U.S. government was not only complicit in the attacks but orchestrated them to fulfill a long-term agenda of control and domination. Theories such as controlled demolition, the stand down, and financial manipulation persist because they are grounded in facts that the official narrative fails to address. The evidence is clear: the attacks on 9/11 were a premeditated, calculated operation designed to reshape the global order and strip away individual freedoms, and the only question left is who was at the top pulling the strings.

Those in power have deliberately suppressed the truth behind 9/11, but the evidence is overwhelming that this was an inside job—an orchestrated false flag operation designed to manipulate the public and advance a global agenda of control. It is time to reject the lies and demand accountability from the real perpetrators of this atrocity. The full story of 9/11 has yet to be revealed, and the quest for truth continues as more pieces of the puzzle come to light. The deeper we dig, the clearer it becomes that we have only scratched the surface of this dark and far-reaching conspiracy.

The Epstein Case: Beyond the Headlines

Jeffrey Epstein's life is a tale of meteoric rise and dark secrets. Born in Brooklyn in 1953, Epstein's early career began as a teacher at the Dalton School in Manhattan, where he mingled with the children of influential families. This position opened doors to the world of finance, leading him to a job at Bear Stearns, a major investment bank. Epstein's acumen in financial matters quickly became apparent, and he soon transitioned to managing the wealth of the ultra-rich. By the 1980s, Epstein had established his firm, J. Epstein & Co., catering exclusively to billionaires. He amassed significant wealth through this venture and cultivated connections with high-profile individuals in politics, business, and entertainment. His client list reportedly included the likes of Leslie Wexner, the billionaire founder of L Brands, and former presidents Bill Clinton and Donald Trump. These connections granted Epstein access to the upper echelons of society, where he hosted lavish parties and maintained a jet-setting lifestyle.

However, Epstein's rise to prominence was marred by a series of legal issues and allegations long before his 2019 arrest. In 2005, police in Palm Beach, Florida, began investigating Epstein following reports that he had molested a 14-year-old girl at his mansion. This inquiry uncovered a pattern of abuse involving numerous underage girls. Despite the gravity of the allegations, Epstein managed to negotiate a controversial plea deal in 2008. He pled guilty to state charges of soliciting prostitution from a minor and served only 13 months in a county jail, during which he was allowed to leave for work six days a week. This lenient sentence, orchestrated by then-U.S. Attorney Alexander Acosta, drew sharp criticism and renewed scrutiny over the years.

Epstein's 2019 arrest marked a dramatic turn in his story. On July 6, 2019, he was apprehended at Teterboro Airport in New Jersey on federal charges of sex trafficking minors. The indictment alleged that Epstein operated a vast network of recruiters and victims, luring underage girls to his residences in New York and Florida under the guise of providing massages. These sessions often escalated to sexual abuse. Epstein's arrest set off a media frenzy as his connections to powerful figures and the scope of his alleged crimes came under intense examination. Just over a month later, on August 10, 2019, Epstein was found dead in his cell at the Metropolitan Correctional Center in New York. The official ruling was suicide by hanging, but the circumstances of his death raised immediate questions. Reports of broken cameras, understaffed guards, and lapses in security protocols fueled suspicions. Reports stating that Epstein had attempted suicide weeks earlier and was subsequently removed from suicide watch only heightened the intrigue.

The broader implications of the Epstein case are profound. It has significantly raised public awareness of human trafficking and exploitation, shining a spotlight on the vulnerabilities of underage victims and the mechanisms predators use to exploit them. The case has also eroded trust in the criminal justice system. Many view Epstein's initial plea deal and the circumstances surrounding his death as evidence of a system that protects the powerful at the expense of justice. This perception fuels a sense of cynicism and disillusionment with the institutions meant to uphold the law.

Furthermore, the Epstein case has sparked critical discussions about power, privilege, and accountability. It has highlighted how wealth and influence can be used to evade consequences and manipulate legal outcomes. The case continues to resonate in public discourse, prompting calls for greater transparency and reforms to prevent similar abuses of power. Jeffrey Epstein's story is a stark reminder of the dark intersections between wealth, influence, and criminality, impacting society's quest for justice and truth.

A Legacy of Global Corruption and Elite Control

The official account of Jeffrey Epstein's life and crimes obscures a deeper, systemic truth: Epstein was not merely an individual acting alone, but a key player in a network designed to secure leverage over influential figures worldwide. His connections to intelligence circles and elite social spheres reveal an operation with roots in global control and manipulation. The following sections examine his ties to powerful agencies, influential personalities, and events leading to his demise—all interconnected elements of a far-reaching agenda driven by those in the shadows.

The Intelligence Allegations

One of the most enduring theories surrounding Jeffrey Epstein is his connection to intelligence agencies, either in the U.S. or abroad. Epstein's ability to evade serious legal consequences for decades, despite overwhelming accusations, points to covert protection from powerful interests. It's no coincidence that Epstein had relationships with influential figures across the political and corporate spectrum. The true scope of Epstein's operation was far more than just personal gain; it was part of a complex network designed to gather and weaponize compromising information on global elites.

Epstein's infamous private island and "Lolita Express" jet were not just symbols of excess—they were tools in a well-orchestrated scheme to entrap powerful individuals. Epstein's wealth and connections weren't simply status symbols; they were instruments for blackmail. The notion that Epstein was a covert operative working to amass damaging material on high-profile figures isn't just speculative—it's a vital part of understanding how he remained untouchable for so long. The lack of official acknowledgment of Epstein's ties to intelligence agencies only reinforces the idea that his network reached the highest levels of global power.

The Role of Powerful Figures in His Death

Epstein's close relationships with some of the world's most powerful people go far beyond mere social connections—they reveal the heart of a much larger operation. Epstein was not just a manipulative predator; he was a key figure in an international web of corruption, where he held evidence that could expose global elites involved in illicit activities. The fact that Epstein's associates included royalty, politicians, and corporate titans is no coincidence. His death, far from being a simple suicide, was a calculated move to protect these powerful figures from exposure.

The lapses in jail security, malfunctioning cameras, and conveniently timed "errors" during Epstein's final hours scream of foul play. Epstein had in his possession evidence—videos, photographs, documents—capable of bringing down some of the most influential people on the planet. His death was not a failure of the system; it was a deliberate assassination, orchestrated to prevent him from striking a deal and exposing the dark secrets of the elite. This was not an isolated incident but part of a larger effort to suppress the truth and protect those who pull the strings behind the scenes.

The notion that Epstein committed suicide is a transparent cover-up designed to silence the most damning witness in modern history. Epstein's knowledge of the global trafficking network, and his connections to the political and corporate elite, posed too much of a risk. His death was far too convenient, and the circumstances surrounding it too suspicious to be ignored. From malfunctioning cameras to the guards who "fell asleep," everything points to an assassination carried out with precision and intent.

Epstein was silenced because he knew too much, and his death served one purpose: to protect the powerful individuals tied to his criminal network. The cover-up was sloppy, but the message was clear—those in power will go to any lengths to protect themselves. This extends beyond mere speculation; it's bolstered by inconsistencies and glaring oversights in the official investigation that hint at a coordinated effort to obscure the truth. The idea that Epstein's death was a coordinated hit orchestrated by the elite is not only plausible—it's the only explanation that fits the facts.

Epstein's Global Network

Epstein wasn't acting alone. He was a critical node in a vast global network of human trafficking, exploitation, and blackmail that reaches into the highest echelons of power. This wasn't a simple case of one man's depravity—it was an international conspiracy, implicating global elites in some of the most heinous crimes imaginable. Epstein's wealth and connections were not just personal assets; they were part of a criminal enterprise involving money laundering, political corruption, and exploitation on a global scale.

From members of the British Royal Family to high-ranking politicians and business leaders, Epstein's network reveals the interconnectedness of global elites and their involvement in dark, illegal activities. The evidence of this international trafficking ring has been systematically buried, but the connections between Epstein and some of the most powerful figures in the world are undeniable. The global elite used Epstein as a tool to advance their nefarious agenda, and when he became a liability, they eliminated him.

Systemic Failure and Corruption

The corruption surrounding Epstein's case is not just about one man's ability to escape justice—it's a glaring example of how deeply embedded the global elite are within the legal and political systems. Epstein's sweetheart plea deal in 2008 and his eventual "suicide" reveal a justice system that works to protect the rich and powerful, not hold them accountable. The fact that his contact list—potentially a window into a world of illicit dealings and high-profile associations—remains unseen exemplifies the lengths taken to keep the truth hidden.

The system wasn't just manipulated by Epstein—it was complicit in his crimes. The global elite's control over intelligence, law enforcement, and the courts is why Epstein could operate so freely and why he was silenced before the full scope of his network could come to light. His case is a clear window into the workings of the Deep State, the shadowy network of global elites and government operatives pulling strings behind the scenes. As we examine the Deep State's broader influence, it becomes impossible to ignore how Epstein's life and death reflect the systematic control exerted by the global elite. Epstein was silenced to protect a network that continues to shape world events from the shadows.

The Deep State: A Hidden Government?

The concept of the "Deep State" has become a prevalent topic in political discourse, particularly in recent years. The term refers to a supposed network of unelected officials and bureaucrats who secretly manipulate or control government policy and decision-making, operating independently of elected representatives. Although the term gained traction in the United States, it originates in political discussions in Turkey, where it was used to describe clandestine networks within the state, including military and intelligence officials acting autonomously. In other countries, similar concepts exist but are often referred to using different terminologies. What sets the idea of the Deep State apart from regular bureaucratic processes is its implication of a hidden agenda and covert operations, distinct from government agencies' transparent and accountable functions.

Proponents of the Deep State theory argue that this hidden government works behind the scenes to undermine elected officials and influence policy in ways that serve its interests rather than those of the public. They allege that unelected bureaucrats manipulate elected leaders, ensuring that certain policies remain unchanged regardless of who is in office. Claims of coordinated efforts to sabotage or discredit political figures, particularly those who challenge the status quo, are central to this theory. Supporters often cite leaked documents and whistleblower testimonies as evidence of these covert operations. For instance, they point to internal communications within government agencies or intelligence reports suggesting a level of orchestration beyond publicly acknowledged.

Critically evaluating the evidence for and against the Deep State theory reveals a complex landscape. Specific incidents often cited as proof of Deep State activity include high-profile leaks and internal conflicts within the government. For example, the release of classified information by whistleblowers like Edward Snowden or the friction between intelligence agencies and political leaders during various administrations are seen by some as indicators of a Deep State at work. However, a closer examination of these incidents often shows a more nuanced reality. Intelligence agencies' role and influence on government policy is significant, but it is not necessarily evidence of a coordinated conspiracy. These agencies operate under a mandate to protect national security, and their actions, while sometimes controversial, are usually subject to oversight and legal constraints.

Counterarguments from political scientists and experts often emphasize the inherent complexity of governmental operations. They argue that what is perceived as Deep State activity is more likely the result of bureaucratic inertia, inter-agency competition, and the challenges of implementing policy in a large, multifaceted government. These experts point out that the checks and balances built into democratic systems are designed to prevent any single group from gaining unchecked power. While there may be instances of overreach or misconduct, attributing them to a monolithic Deep State oversimplifies the reality of governance.

The impact of the Deep State theory on contemporary politics is substantial. It has profoundly shaped political campaigns and rhetoric, with candidates and elected officials using the term to rally support and discredit opponents. The idea of a hidden government working against the will of the people resonates with those who feel disenfranchised or mistrustful of established institutions. This rhetoric can galvanize voter bases and polarize public opinion, making constructive dialogue more challenging. The theory has also affected voter trust and engagement. Belief in a Deep State can lead to cynicism and apathy, as citizens may feel that their votes and voices have little impact on the actual functioning of government. This erosion of trust undermines the democratic process and can lead to decreased participation in elections and civic activities.

Media plays a crucial role in perpetuating or debunking the Deep State theory. News outlets and social media platforms amplify narratives that align with their audiences' beliefs, creating echo chambers where these ideas can flourish. Sensationalized reporting on government scandals, leaks, and internal conflicts can feed into the perception of a Deep State, even when the underlying issues are more complex. Conversely, investigative journalism and fact-checking efforts strive to provide a balanced perspective, highlighting the lack of concrete evidence for a coordinated hidden government while acknowledging legitimate concerns about transparency and accountability.

Unveiling the Hidden Hand of Power
The Deep State, in general, is not a theory—it's the reality of how global power operates. Beneath the surface of elected governments, an unelected group of powerful individuals—spanning intelligence agencies, military leadership, corporate elites, and secretive organizations—controls policies and decisions, overriding the authority of elected officials. This shadow network doesn't merely influence government; it dictates the direction of global politics, ensuring that their agenda is always advanced, regardless of public will or democratic processes.

This hidden network uses its immense influence to maintain control over economies, resources, and global events, manipulating public perception and orchestrating outcomes that serve its interests. Intelligence operations, financial markets, and even international conflicts are used as tools to perpetuate the power of this elite class. The true purpose of the Deep State is to consolidate wealth, suppress dissent, and create an illusion of choice, driving toward a globalist new world order where real power remains in the hands of a select few.

<u>Control Through Conflicts and Crisis</u>
The evidence for the Deep State's existence is seen in the undeniable influence of intelligence agencies and defense contractors on major global events. The U.S. military's endless involvement in the Middle East is not driven by national security concerns but by the profit motives of defense contractors and control over vital oil interests. The wars in Iraq and Afghanistan were engineered not for protection, but as part of a larger strategy to expand the military-industrial complex's profits while securing critical resources for the global elite. Halliburton, Lockheed Martin, and other defense giants made billions from these conflicts—conflicts initiated and sustained by the Deep State, not by public interest.

This pattern of manipulation doesn't end with military intervention. The 2008 financial crisis is another glaring example of the Deep State at work. As millions of people lost their homes, jobs, and life savings, major banks like Goldman Sachs and AIG were handed billion-dollar bailouts—paid for by taxpayers. This was not a rescue effort for the economy; it was a calculated move to protect the global financial elite at the expense of ordinary citizens. The Deep State used the crisis to further enrich themselves while the public was left to suffer the consequences.

The Deep State's Enforcers

The Deep State doesn't just wield power through corporations and defense contractors—it exerts control through the intelligence apparatus. Whistleblowers like Edward Snowden and Julian Assange revealed what many have long suspected: that intelligence agencies operate with impunity, manipulating global events from behind the scenes. The NSA, CIA, and other agencies aren't merely tools of national security—they are the enforcers of the Deep State's agenda.

The surveillance programs exposed by Snowden were not designed to protect against terrorism but to monitor and control the populace, keeping potential dissent in check. Assange's WikiLeaks revelations laid bare the corruption within governments, exposing how intelligence agencies collude with political elites to undermine democracy and maintain the status quo. These agencies operate with little to no oversight, proving that real power does not lie with elected officials but with the shadow network that controls them.

Sabotaging Threats to the Deep State

Those who dare to expose or challenge the Deep State are systematically discredited, sabotaged, or removed from power. Political figures and whistleblowers who threaten to reveal the truth about this hidden network often find themselves the targets of smear campaigns, legal battles, or worse. Media leaks, scandals, and orchestrated attacks are just some of the methods used by the Deep State to neutralize threats to its control.

The fate of these individuals isn't a series of coincidences—it's evidence of a coordinated effort to protect the elite from exposure. Figures like Snowden and Assange are vilified not because of the danger they pose to national security, but because of the threat they pose to the secretive global network that pulls the strings of government. The Deep State will stop at nothing to silence those who might reveal its true nature.

Beyond Speculation

Critics who claim that the Deep State is nothing more than a theory dismiss the overwhelming evidence of this network's influence. The pattern of events—manipulated wars, financial crises that enrich the elite, and the suppression of those who dare to speak out—proves that the Deep State is not an oversimplification or bureaucratic inertia. It's a well-orchestrated, ongoing conspiracy to ensure the interests of the few over the needs of the many.

The Deep State's influence isn't bound by checks and balances—it operates outside the law, and its power is rarely contested. This secretive network of elites works tirelessly to shape global politics, ensuring that they remain immune from accountability. The evidence is everywhere: intelligence agencies that manipulate political outcomes, defense contractors that profit from orchestrated conflicts, and financial elites that grow richer while the rest of the world suffers under the weight of their decisions.

A Global Agenda for Control
The Deep State doesn't just influence governments—it controls the direction of global affairs, pushing forward an agenda that serves the interests of a few globalist elites. This hidden power structure transcends borders, weaving together intelligence agencies, multinational corporations, and secretive organizations resembling the Illuminati. Their goals are clear: to consolidate power, control global resources, and suppress any movements that threaten their dominance.

For those who remain skeptical, consider this: the evidence suggests that the Deep State's existence is not just circumstantial—it's written in the policies and outcomes of the world's most significant events. The wars in the Middle East, the global financial crises, and the suppression of whistleblowers can all be seen as pointing to a coordinated effort by powerful actors operating behind the scenes. This isn't merely a matter of belief but a perspective based on patterns that many interpret as signs of a hidden influence.

The proof of the Deep State's influence lies in the high-profile events that have shaped global politics and economics. These are not random occurrences but carefully orchestrated moves by those in power. Two of the clearest examples of the Deep State's reach are the U.S. invasion of Iraq and the 2008 global financial crisis, both of which reveal the deep connections between elites, corporations, and government agencies working behind the scenes.

The Iraq War and Military-Industrial Complex
The U.S. invasion of Iraq in 2003 stands as one of the most glaring examples of the Deep State at work. The decision to go to war was not driven by the threat posed by Iraq but by the interests of the military-industrial complex—a powerful network of defense contractors, military leaders, and government officials. This war, orchestrated behind the

scenes, served to enrich defense companies like Halliburton and Lockheed Martin, who profited massively from government contracts tied to military operations.

The justification for the invasion was based on deliberately falsified intelligence about weapons of mass destruction (WMDs), a fabrication used to manipulate the public and create the pretext for war. Intelligence agencies played a pivotal role in spreading this misinformation, colluding with defense contractors to promote their shared agendas, all while disregarding the true interests of the public. This was no accident—this was a calculated move by the Deep State to expand its influence, secure resources, and fuel the profits of the military-industrial complex.

The Iraq War exemplifies how the Deep State manipulates foreign policy for financial gain, keeping the public in the dark while pushing forward an agenda that benefits only the elite. The immense profits made by defense contractors, coupled with the lack of accountability for the deception surrounding WMDs, only further proves that this war was a product of the Deep State's control over global affairs.

The 2008 Financial Crisis and Wall Street Bailouts
The 2008 financial crisis is another prime example of the Deep State's manipulation of global events for the benefit of the elite. As millions of ordinary citizens lost their homes, jobs, and savings, the U.S. government stepped in to protect the true beneficiaries of the system—Wall Street banks and financial institutions. Companies like Goldman Sachs, AIG, and Bank of America received billions in taxpayer-funded bailouts, orchestrated by the same financial elites who caused the collapse in the first place.

This was not a response to protect the economy—it was a coordinated effort by the Deep State to safeguard the interests of the wealthy and powerful, leaving the public to bear the consequences of their greed. The revolving door between Wall Street and key government positions, with former Goldman Sachs executives taking control of the Treasury, exemplifies how deeply entrenched the financial elite is in government. This rigged system is designed to ensure that no matter what happens, the wealthy are protected, while the average person suffers.

The bailouts were nothing more than a cover to allow the financial elite to retain their wealth and power, with no significant consequences for those responsible for the crisis. This is the hallmark of Deep State control: the powerful manipulating government policy to ensure they remain untouched by the chaos they create, while the public is forced to endure the fallout.

The Iraq War and the 2008 financial crisis are not isolated events—they suggest a more broad, orchestrated effort by the Deep State to maintain global control and enrich the globalist elite at the expense of the public. These high-profile examples demonstrate how the Deep State operates in plain sight, using conflict, crisis, and manipulation to achieve its goals. As we examine these events more closely, it becomes clear that the Deep State's hand is present in nearly every significant global event, shaping the future in ways that benefit only those in power.

Chapter 6

Conspiracies in Science and Technology

Imagine standing on the surface of the Moon, looking at the Earth, a blue and white marble floating in the vastness of space. The idea that humans actually made it to the Moon is awe-inspiring. Yet, despite overwhelming evidence, some still believe it never happened. The Moon Landing Hoax theory persists, igniting debates and skepticism. Let's get to the context, claims, and evidence surrounding one of the most famous conspiracies in modern history.

The Moon Landing: Triumph or Illusion?

The Moon landing on July 20, 1969, stands as one of humanity's greatest achievements, driven by the fierce space race between the United States and the Soviet Union. This rivalry intensified after World War II, as both superpowers competed to assert their dominance in technology and space exploration. When the Soviet Union launched Sputnik, the world's first artificial satellite, in 1957, it catalyzed American efforts to take the lead. In 1961, President John F. Kennedy challenged the United States to put a man on the Moon and bring him back safely before the end of the decade. His bold vision was both a scientific and symbolic commitment, intended to showcase American ingenuity and technological superiority.

To fulfill Kennedy's challenge, NASA launched the Apollo program, drawing on the expertise of thousands of engineers, scientists, and astronauts. The program was a tremendous national effort involving extensive testing and numerous missions to ensure the safety and success of a lunar landing. The Apollo missions included both unmanned and manned missions to test spacecraft systems, life-support mechanisms, and the technical challenges of orbiting and landing on the Moon.

Apollo 1, the first manned mission, tragically ended in a cabin fire during a ground test, killing all three astronauts on board. However, NASA pressed on, using this setback to improve safety standards and refine mission protocols. Subsequent missions, including Apollo 8, which orbited the Moon, and Apollo 10, which performed a close approach without landing, paved the way for a successful lunar landing.

On July 16, 1969, Apollo 11 launched with astronauts Neil Armstrong, Buzz Aldrin, and Michael Collins. The story goes that four days later, the lunar module, known as the Eagle, separated from the command module and descended toward the Moon. With Armstrong piloting, the Eagle touched down in the Sea of Tranquility, and at 10:56 PM EDT, Armstrong descended the ladder, making him the first human to set foot on the Moon. His iconic words, "That's one small step for man, one giant leap for mankind," resonated with millions worldwide, capturing the moment's historical significance.

It's said that Aldrin soon joined Armstrong on the lunar surface, where the two spent over two hours collecting rock samples, taking photographs, and deploying scientific instruments, including a seismometer and a laser reflector to measure the exact distance between the Earth and the Moon. Meanwhile, Collins piloted the command module in lunar orbit, maintaining critical communication links with the astronauts below.

After completing their tasks on the Moon, Armstrong and Aldrin returned to the command module, where Collins awaited, and the trio began their journey back to Earth. They safely landed in the Pacific Ocean on July 24, 1969, marking the successful completion of the mission. The Apollo 11 mission not only fulfilled Kennedy's vision but also ushered in an era of scientific discovery and technological progress that would inspire future space exploration efforts.

If it happened, the Moon landing demonstrated unprecedented human cooperation, resilience, and innovation. The program's successes led to further Apollo missions, which conducted more scientific research on the Moon's surface and brought back samples for study. The data gathered continues to inform lunar science and planetary exploration, setting the groundwork for future missions to other celestial bodies. Today, the Apollo 11 mission is celebrated as a monumental accomplishment in human history and a testament to the possibilities unlocked through exploration and scientific pursuit.

The Truth They Don't Want You to Know

The Apollo Moon landings have long been touted as one of humanity's greatest achievements, but a growing body of evidence suggests otherwise. Far from a groundbreaking mission, the Moon landing was an elaborate hoax orchestrated to maintain U.S. dominance in the Space Race. Figures like Bart Sibrel have dedicated years to exposing the reality behind the Apollo program, revealing it as nothing more than a carefully staged spectacle. NASA, under immense pressure from the government and public, needed to win the race to the Moon—but rather than achieve this through genuine exploration, they manufactured the entire event on Earth.

Proof of Staging

A glaring piece of evidence often overlooked is the recording of the astronauts' exit from the lunar module. How could the camera be perfectly positioned outside the shuttle, already capturing their descent onto the lunar surface? This implies that the scene was pre-arranged and filmed in a controlled environment. NASA's silence on this inexplicable detail speaks volumes, adding yet another layer to the ever-mounting proof that the footage was staged.

Defying Space Physics

One of the most iconic images from the so-called Moon landing is Neil Armstrong and Buzz Aldrin planting the American flag on the lunar surface. But, in the footage, the flag flutters as though caught in a breeze—an impossibility in the vacuum of space where there's no air. NASA's flimsy excuse that a horizontal rod was used to keep the flag extended, and that the movement came from the astronauts twisting it into the ground, fails to convince. The movement of the flag is one of the clearest indicators that the event was filmed on Earth, likely in a studio where wind could easily explain the fluttering flag.

Film Set Giveaways

Another key piece of evidence supporting the hoax theory lies in the lighting and shadows seen in the footage. Photographs and videos from the Apollo missions show shadows falling in different directions, inconsistent with a single light source like the sun. This is a clear sign of multiple artificial light sources, as would be used on a movie set. NASA claims the uneven surface of the Moon caused these discrepancies, but that explanation doesn't hold up when you examine the precision of the shadows. These irregularities, along with the professional film quality, suggest that studio lights were employed to recreate the scene. After all, creating the illusion of a lunar landscape would have required extensive lighting manipulation.

A Barrier to the Moon

One of the most damning pieces of evidence that the Moon landing never happened is the existence of the Van Allen radiation belts. These zones of intense radiation encircle Earth, and any spacecraft attempting to pass through them would expose its crew to deadly doses of radiation. NASA's claim that the Apollo missions were timed to minimize exposure, and that the spacecraft had adequate shielding, is laughable at best. No human could survive the journey through these belts in the technology of the 1960s. This is a critical flaw in the official narrative, proving that the missions were impossible from the start.

A Staged Set

Ever notice the absence of stars in the photos and videos taken from the Moon's surface? In the vacuum of space, without an atmosphere to scatter light, stars should have been brilliantly visible. But in the Apollo footage, the stars are conspicuously missing. NASA's excuse? They claim the cameras were set to capture the brightly lit lunar surface, making the distant stars too dim to appear. Yet this is nothing more than an excuse to cover up the truth—studio lights illuminating a set could never replicate the vastness of space, which is why stars are absent in every image and video from the supposed Moon landing.

Buzz Aldrin's Confession

Buzz Aldrin himself provided perhaps the most striking piece of evidence supporting the hoax theory. In a recorded interview, Aldrin was quoted as saying that they never went to the Moon—a confession that was conveniently ignored by mainstream media. His statements, combined with his evasive and sometimes defensive behavior in interviews, further point to the astronauts' knowledge of the cover-up. Aldrin's physical altercation with Bart Sibrel after being confronted about the hoax only deepens suspicions. Why would a man who achieved such a monumental feat react with violence if he had nothing to hide?

The Perfect Cover-Up

If the Moon landings were real, why would NASA "lose" its original data regarding the Apollo missions? This critical information, including telemetry data, has mysteriously disappeared, conveniently making it impossible to verify the original mission claims. How can such vital information be lost if it truly documented one of the greatest human achievements? I'll tell you how. The loss of this data isn't an accident—it's an intentional act of suppression, ensuring that no one can ever definitively disprove the hoax. NASA's inability to produce the data needed to refute the hoax theory only strengthens the argument that the landings were faked.

The Limits of 1960s Technology

In the 1960s, the technological capabilities simply did not exist to land a man on the Moon and safely return him to Earth. The computers on board the Apollo spacecraft were far too rudimentary to manage such a complex mission. NASA's claims that they were able to guide astronauts through space with less computing power than a modern-day calculator are absurd. The entire mission—from launch to landing—was beyond the technological limits of the time. This is why the Moon landing was staged: it was the only way to "win" the Space Race without risking failure.

A Fabricated Victory

The U.S. government needed a victory in the Space Race to assert its dominance over the Soviet Union. Staging a Moon landing was the easiest way to achieve this without risking the embarrassment of failure. The Apollo program wasn't about scientific discovery—it was about optics and Cold War propaganda. By faking the Moon landing, the U.S. was able to maintain its technological superiority without ever leaving Earth's atmosphere.

The Hoax is Clear

The evidence overwhelmingly supports the conclusion that the Moon landing was staged. From the inconsistencies in the footage, the technical impossibilities, and the suspicious behavior of those involved, significant doubt is cast on the official story. It appears that NASA, with support from the U.S. government, orchestrated an elaborate narrative to solidify its position as a global superpower. As more people question the established account, the truth behind the Moon landing is coming to light.

Contrails or Chemtrails?

High above our heads, silvery threads weave through the azure canvas of our sky, leaving patterns that have sparked both scientific inquiry and boundless speculation. These atmospheric phenomena, officially documented as condensation trails or "contrails," have become the subject of intense scrutiny among researchers and observers alike. While the official narrative provides a seemingly straightforward explanation for these persistent aerial formations, a deeper examination of their behavior raises questions that merit further investigation.

From a purely meteorological standpoint, these vapor trails emerge when aircraft traverse the upper troposphere, where temperatures typically plunge below -40°C. Here, aircraft engines release hot exhaust containing water vapor into the frigid atmosphere, creating visible condensation trails that can persist under specific atmospheric conditions. However, the striking variation in the longevity and dispersion patterns of these trails has led many observers to question whether traditional atmospheric physics alone can explain their behavior.

Modern air traffic has increased dramatically since the 1990s, coinciding with a notable shift in the characteristics of these aerial phenomena. While conventional meteorological models attribute the persistence of these trails to varying humidity levels and wind patterns at high altitudes, some atmospheric scientists have noted unusual particulate compositions in high-altitude air samples that seem to defy traditional explanations.

The official documentation from aviation authorities maintains that these trails consist purely of water vapor and standard engine exhaust. Yet, the presence of certain metallic compounds in upper atmosphere samples—officially attributed to normal fuel combustion—has raised eyebrows among environmental researchers. These particles, including aluminum oxide and barium compounds, appear in concentrations that some independent researchers suggest warrant closer examination.

What makes this phenomenon particularly intriguing is the apparent correlation between increased trail activity and specific atmospheric conditions. While weather manipulation programs like cloud seeding are openly acknowledged by governmental agencies, the full scope of atmospheric engineering capabilities remains surprisingly classified. This intersection of known scientific principles and restricted information creates a fascinating gray area where speculation flourishes in the absence of complete transparency.

The evolution of aviation technology has paralleled these atmospheric changes, with modern aircraft utilizing increasingly sophisticated fuel mixtures and engine designs. These advancements, while documented in broad strokes, often involve proprietary technologies protected by both corporate interests and national security protocols. This veil of secrecy, while potentially necessary for competitive and security reasons, has inadvertently created an information vacuum that begs to be filled.

The Truth Behind the Spray

Now that you know the official narrative behind these trails, let's understand why they are more likely chemicals than condensation. Let's start with calling them what they are: Chemtrails. Despite years of assurances from authorities, mounting evidence suggests these trails are far from harmless condensation—they represent a disturbing and deliberate program, concealed in plain sight, with potentially serious implications for public health and the environment. These trails are seen as part of a deliberate and coordinated effort to spray toxic chemicals into the atmosphere for purposes ranging from weather manipulation to population control.

The evidence for Chemtrails is overwhelming. It starts with what we can see with our own eyes: grids and crisscross patterns in the sky that linger far longer than any natural contrail ever should. These formations aren't the result of regular air traffic. The organized and systematic nature of these trails is a clear indication that something far more deliberate is taking place—something that official sources refuse to acknowledge.

The Proof is in the Particles
For those still in doubt, consider the hard evidence: soil and water samples collected after heavy Chemtrail spraying show dangerously elevated levels of barium, aluminum, and strontium—metals that should not exist in such high concentrations naturally. This is no coincidence. These chemicals are being intentionally introduced into the atmosphere, and their presence correlates directly with the areas experiencing heavy Chemtrail activity.

These metals aren't harmless. Numerous health problems—including respiratory illnesses, asthma spikes, and other chronic conditions—are reported in areas where Chemtrails are most commonly sighted. The health effects are undeniable, and for many who live under the cloud of constant Chemtrail spraying, the impact is deeply personal. The government's silence on this issue only further suggests that something is being covered up.

Weather Manipulation and Government Secrecy
Beyond health concerns, Chemtrails can also be tied to weather manipulation. After intense Chemtrail activity, there are reports of unusual weather patterns—dramatic temperature drops, unnatural cloud formations, and even localized storms. These are not natural occurrences. The deliberate alteration of weather through spraying is a powerful tool in the hands of those seeking to control resources and populations.

Let's not forget that governments have a history of engaging in covert operations without public knowledge. Projects like MKUltra, Operation Popeye, and countless other classified operations have proven that governments are willing and able to manipulate the public for their own agendas. Chemtrails are just another chapter in this ongoing saga of control, deceit, and manipulation. The fact that they deny it so vehemently only further validates foul play.

The Reality on the Ground
For many of the affected, Chemtrails are not just a distant theory—they are a daily reality. People have witnessed the spraying firsthand, noticed unusual illnesses in their communities, and experienced sudden changes in the environment that coincide with

heavy Chemtrail activity. They don't see these as random events—they see them as direct results of toxic chemicals being introduced into the atmosphere.

Those who have seen inside the planes used for these operations, those who have taken samples, and those who suffer the consequences firsthand know that Chemtrails are no longer up for debate. To them, the evidence is clear, the effects are real, and the cover-up is massive. Official denials cannot erase the substantial evidence supporting Chemtrails as a global tool of control and manipulation.

Unmasking the Truth

The time for skepticism is over. Chemtrails are not just a theory—they are a reality, backed by overwhelming evidence and countless personal testimonies from those who have experienced their effects firsthand. Soil and water samples showing elevated levels of harmful chemicals, unusual weather patterns following heavy spraying, and the rising number of unexplained health issues all point to a deliberate, coordinated effort to introduce dangerous substances into our atmosphere. The refusal of governments and mainstream institutions to acknowledge or address this issue only confirms their role in concealing the truth. It falls upon those brave enough to see through the deception to continue exposing the truth behind Chemtrails and hold those responsible accountable for the damage being done to our planet and our health.

HAARP's Hidden Power

In the remote wilderness of Gakona, Alaska, the High-Frequency Active Auroral Research Program (HAARP) stands as a key facility in the study of the ionosphere. Established in 1993 through a collaboration involving the U.S. Air Force, the U.S. Navy, and the Defense Advanced Research Projects Agency (DARPA), HAARP's primary objective is to enhance our understanding of this atmospheric layer, which plays a critical role in communication and navigation systems.

HAARP features a sophisticated array of antennas known as the Ionospheric Research Instrument (IRI), capable of sending high-frequency radio waves into the ionosphere. These radio waves interact with charged particles in the ionosphere, allowing researchers to investigate phenomena such as auroras, radio wave propagation, and the effects of solar activity on communication systems.

The program has undergone rigorous testing, leading to important advancements in scientific research. By studying the ionosphere, HAARP contributes to better satellite communication and navigation, improving the reliability of GPS systems. Furthermore, the data gathered aids in predicting and mitigating the impact of space weather on technological infrastructures, providing valuable insights for both military and civilian applications.

While HAARP's scientific objectives are clear, the program's operations and findings are often conducted within a framework of national security. This aspect has led to public intrigue and scrutiny, with the facility frequently discussed in the context of geoengineering and other speculative theories. Nevertheless, its disclosed mission remains focused on legitimate atmospheric research aimed at enhancing our technological capabilities and understanding of the Earth's atmosphere.

As a product of ongoing technological advancements, HAARP reflects the evolving nature of atmospheric research. The complexities of the ionosphere are increasingly relevant, especially given the challenges posed by climate change and the demand for reliable communication systems. Officially, HAARP is intended to enhance scientific understanding of atmospheric phenomena, positioning itself as a key contributor to the future of atmospheric research.

The Undeniable Weapon of Control

Now that you have heard the official narrative let's talk about HAARP's true capabilities, which extend far beyond the benign scientific research. The facility in Gakona is not just a research tool—it is a powerful and secretive weapon, designed for manipulation on a global scale. For those who have dug into the facts, HAARP's potential to affect weather, manipulate minds, and even control populations is not a theory—it's a reality backed by a disturbing body of evidence. Why else would the government keep HAARP so secretive, with restricted public access and minimal oversight, if not to hide its real purpose? This facility isn't about understanding the ionosphere; it's about controlling the world.

Weather Manipulation and Disaster Creation

HAARP is widely believed to have the ability to influence natural disasters, causing hurricanes, earthquakes, and other weather phenomena at will. There are numerous "coincidences" between HAARP's operational timeline and several devastating natural disasters, like the 2010 Haiti earthquake and Hurricane Katrina. These events might not be mere acts of nature, but deliberate uses of HAARP's technology to create chaos and destabilize regions. The increase in intensity and frequency of these disasters since HAARP's inception is too suspicious to ignore. This is further supported by HAARP's technology, which can easily be used to manipulate the ionosphere and disrupt weather systems, triggering catastrophic events under the guise of natural disasters, leaving no trace of human interference.

Electromagnetic Warfare and Mind Control

HAARP's reach goes even further than controlling the weather. The facility is suspected of engaging in electromagnetic warfare, targeting brainwaves to control the masses. It is not unreasonable to believe that HAARP can be used to generate waves that alter moods, behaviors, and even thoughts, turning populations into passive, easily controlled subjects. The notion of using such technology for mind control may sound far-fetched to some, but with the advancements in technology we know exist today, it's hardly beyond the realm of possibility. After all, if the government has the means to manipulate weather, why wouldn't they also use it to manipulate the people?

Geopolitical Domination Through Disaster

HAARP's potential role in geopolitical warfare is another aspect that can't be ignored. It is alleged that the U.S. government has weaponized HAARP to target rival nations with devastating weather patterns, from droughts that cripple agricultural production to storms that destroy infrastructure. With the power to cause chaos in any region without leaving a trace, HAARP becomes the perfect weapon of indirect warfare. Whether it's economic sabotage or political destabilization, HAARP gives the U.S. an unparalleled advantage in maintaining global control without the need for conventional military intervention.

Media Manipulation

The documented use of media and television as tools for manipulation and control further supports the idea that HAARP may not be operating in isolation. Television, radio, and media broadcasts can be used in conjunction with HAARP's technology to influence public perception, moods, and behavior. It's no secret that governments have long relied on media to sway public opinion, and the introduction of electromagnetic waves from HAARP could amplify these effects, creating a population that is easily subdued. The mainstream media's refusal to report on HAARP's possible capabilities further solidifies their likely complicity in the cover-up.

The Legal Loophole

There's even more alarming evidence that the government is fully aware of HAARP's power over weather systems. International guidelines have already addressed the issue, stating that HAARP facilities cannot be used to affect other nations' weather patterns. However, by law, the U.S. government is legally permitted to use HAARP's capabilities to influence its own nation's weather. Why would this legal loophole exist if weather manipulation wasn't already happening? This revelation alone supports that the government has no intention of using HAARP solely for "research" but also as a tool for controlling its citizens through engineered weather events.

Why the Secrecy?

If HAARP was truly about scientific research, there would be no need for the extreme secrecy surrounding the facility. The lack of transparency, the restricted access, and the refusal to allow independent oversight all point to one conclusion: HAARP's true purpose is too dangerous to be revealed. Historical precedents like MKUltra and Operation Popeye—both of which were once dismissed as conspiracy theories—have since been proven true. HAARP will likely prove to be no different. The government has a long history of keeping secret programs hidden from the public, and HAARP is simply the latest example of this disturbing trend.

The Tip of the Iceberg

What if the theorists are right, and HAARP isn't just a research facility but a weapon for controlling weather, influencing minds, and securing global dominance? Could this be yet another case of the powerful burying the truth under secrecy? With the capabilities and classified nature of HAARP, this may not be mere speculation but a hidden reality. It's time to look beyond questions—HAARP represents a dangerous shift in governmental power, and this facility could be just one part of a larger agenda to control global events.

What's even more alarming is that HAARP is likely only one of *many* hidden projects designed to manipulate the environment, the population, and global affairs. Governments, intelligence agencies, and elites operate in the shadows, pushing forward a global agenda that relies on secrecy and control. The truth behind HAARP is just the beginning—more must be revealed. Those willing to look beyond the surface are the ones who will ultimately uncover the deeper truths that the public is not meant to see.

CHAPTER 7

MEDIA AND THE SPREAD OF CONSPIRACY THEORIES

JAMIE IS SITTING IN her living room in the early 1960s, flicking through the pages of her daily newspaper. She comes across an article about the assassination of President John F. Kennedy. The piece is filled with speculation, theories, and hints of a larger plot. This was how many Americans first encountered the notion that Kennedy's death might not have been the work of a lone gunman. Traditional media—newspapers, TV, and radio—have long been crucial in shaping public perception and spreading conspiracy theories.

As we explore the world of conspiracy theories, it's important to pause and consider the media's role. While some theories gain traction through speculation and misinformation, traditional media—such as newspapers, television, and radio—often strive to provide facts and context. However, how stories are reported or sensationalized can, in some cases, inadvertently fuel the spread of conspiracy theories. Understanding this dynamic gives us deeper insight into how these ideas are communicated and why they resonate with certain audiences. I'll use the term "theories" throughout this chapter for simplicity, but let's be clear: the media's role in spreading information has not only fueled various claims, but it's also contributed significantly to the public's growing mistrust in official narratives.

The Role of Media in Shaping Perceptions

In the aftermath of JFK's assassination, newspapers played a pivotal role in fueling conspiracy theories. Journalists and columnists speculated about the possibility of multiple shooters, CIA involvement, and Mafia connections. The sheer volume of articles and editorials on the subject created a fertile ground for conspiracy theories to take root. As more details emerged, newspapers continued to feed the public's curiosity, often blurring the line between fact and speculation. This coverage informed the public and shaped their perceptions, leading many to question the official narrative.

Television documentaries and specials have also played a significant role in popular-izing conspiracy theories. Programs like "The Men Who Killed Kennedy" and "JFK: The Smoking Gun" brought complex theories to a broad audience, using visuals and expert testimonies to create compelling narratives. These documentaries often combined historical footage with dramatic reenactments, making the theories seem more plausible. The impact of such programs is profound, as they reach millions of viewers and leave last-ing impressions. They provide a platform for alternative perspectives, often challenging official accounts and encouraging viewers to think critically about historical events.

Radio shows like "Coast to Coast AM" have become cultural touchstones within the conspiracy theory community. Hosted by figures like Art Bell and George Noory, the show has explored topics ranging from UFOs to government cover-ups. Its late-night time slot and open lines for callers create an intimate and engaging atmosphere where listeners feel like part of a community seeking hidden truths. The show's influence extends beyond entertainment, shaping the beliefs and attitudes of its audience. "Coast to Coast AM" has played a crucial role in mainstreaming conspiracy culture by providing a forum for fringe theories and unconventional ideas.

The rise of social media and online platforms has revolutionized the way conspiracy theo-ries are spread. Platforms like Facebook, Twitter, and YouTube have become the primary vehicles for disseminating these theories. Algorithms designed to maximize engagement often prioritize sensational content, creating echo chambers where conspiracy theories thrive. Viral videos and memes spread misinformation rapidly, reaching millions within hours. The Pizzagate conspiracy, which falsely claimed that a child trafficking ring was being run out of a Washington, D.C. pizzeria, is a stark example. This theory gained traction on alt-right forums and social media, ultimately leading to a real-world armed incident at the Comet Ping Pong pizzeria.

Alternative media and blogs have further contributed to the proliferation of conspiracy theories. Websites like Infowars, founded by Alex Jones, have built large followings by promoting controversial and often unfounded claims. Jones, a prominent conspiracy theorist, has made headlines with his assertions about events like the 9/11 attacks and the Sandy Hook massacre. Infowars has become a hub for alternative narratives, attracting viewers who distrust mainstream media. The influence of such outlets is significant, as they provide a steady stream of content that reinforces the beliefs of their audience.

Independent journalists have also contributed to this landscape. Many have turned to blogging and social media to share their investigations and viewpoints. While some provide valuable insights and challenge official narratives with well-researched arguments, others contribute to misinformation. The line between credible journalism and sensationalist reporting is often blurred, making it challenging for readers to discern the truth.

Studies on media consumption and belief in conspiracies reveal the intricate relationship between the two. Research indicates that frequent use of social media is associated with higher levels of conspiracy thinking. The algorithms that govern these platforms ensure that users are continually exposed to content that aligns with their interests and beliefs. This constant reinforcement makes it difficult for individuals to break free from their echo chambers and consider alternative viewpoints.

The Role of Social Media Algorithms
One critical aspect of the digital age that fuels the spread of conspiracy theories is the role of social media algorithms. Platforms like YouTube, TikTok, Facebook, and Twitter use algorithms designed to prioritize content that generates high levels of engagement. Unfortunately, sensational content often garners more clicks, shares, and comments, leading these algorithms to promote it more frequently. This creates an environment where the most provocative and emotionally charged content rises to the top, regardless of its truthfulness.

For example, YouTube's recommendation system has been widely criticized for content by automatically suggesting similar videos once a user watches one video about a fringe topic. Whether it's content about the flat earth theory, COVID-19 denial, or political conspiracies, YouTube's algorithm can create a rabbit hole effect, pulling users deeper into conspiratorial content by feeding them related videos. Similarly, TikTok's "For You" page algorithm amplifies content based on user interaction, meaning that the more sensational and controversial a video is, the more likely it is to be widely distributed.

These algorithms are designed to keep users on the platform as long as possible by showing them content they're likely to engage with, but they sometimes do so at the expense of factual accuracy. This dynamic has turned social media into fertile ground for the spread of conspiracy theories, as users are continuously exposed to a stream of provocative content that reinforces their existing beliefs. For individuals already predisposed to distrusting mainstream narratives, these algorithms can effectively trap them in echo chambers, where conspiracy theories thrive without challenge.

This algorithmic prioritization of sensationalism is one of the key drivers of why conspiracy theories can gain such rapid traction online. While platforms have made efforts to moderate content and promote fact-checking, the basic design of these systems continues to favor engagement over accuracy. This raises important questions about the responsibility of social media companies to prevent the spread of harmful misinformation while maintaining freedom of expression. It also underscores the importance, as a viewer, of seeking out reliable sources and sharing information that can be supported by fact.

Disinformation and Fake News

In today's digital age, it's crucial to understand the distinctions between disinformation, misinformation, and fake news. Disinformation involves the deliberate spread of false information with the intent to deceive. It's a calculated effort to mislead and manipulate public opinion. Misinformation, on the other hand, is the unintentional spread of incorrect information. People often share misinformation without knowing it's false, believing they spread accurate details. Fake news, a term popularized recently, refers to fabricated news stories explicitly designed to deceive. These stories are often sensational and aim to attract attention or push a particular agenda.

Disinformation campaigns have a long history, dating back to the Cold War. During this period, the United States and the Soviet Union engaged in disinformation to undermine each other's influence. The KGB's Operation INFEKTION, for instance, falsely claimed that the U.S. had created the AIDS virus as a biological weapon. This narrative was spread through forged documents and planted articles in various media outlets, sowing distrust and confusion globally. In the modern era, disinformation has evolved with technology. Social media bots and troll farms amplify false narratives, making them appear more credible and widespread. These automated accounts and organized groups flood platforms with disinformation, manipulating algorithms to ensure that misleading content reaches a broad audience.

The role of disinformation in the 2016 U.S. election is a stark example of its impact. Russian interference through social media campaigns aimed to influence voter behavior and sow discord. Troll farms created divisive content, while bots spread it rapidly across platforms like Facebook and Twitter. These efforts targeted specific demographics with tailored messages, exploiting existing societal tensions. The disinformation campaign was sophisticated, using fake accounts to appear as genuine American citizens. This strategy misled the public and eroded trust in democratic institutions and the electoral process.

Fake news stories significantly influence public perception, often blurring the line between reality and fiction. Prominent phony news stories, such as those claiming that Pope

Francis endorsed Donald Trump or that Hillary Clinton was running a child trafficking ring out of a pizzeria, reached millions of people. These stories were shared widely despite being debunked. The psychological impact of repeated exposure to fake news can be profound. When people see the same false information multiple times, they may begin to believe it, a phenomenon known as the "illusory truth effect." This effect underscores the danger of fake news, as it can solidify false beliefs over time.

The real-world consequences of fake news are alarming. The Pizzagate incident, where a man fired a rifle inside a Washington, D.C. pizzeria because he believed it was the center of a child trafficking ring, highlights the potential for violence fueled by misinformation. Despite being thoroughly debunked, the Pizzagate conspiracy persisted, illustrating how fake news can incite real actions with dangerous outcomes. This incident underscores the importance of addressing fake news and its spread to prevent similar events in the future.

Developing strategies for identifying and counteracting false information is essential to combat disinformation and fake news. Fact-checking websites like Snopes, FactCheck.org, and PolitiFact are invaluable resources. These platforms investigate claims and provide evidence-based conclusions, helping you verify the accuracy of the information you encounter. Additionally, critical thinking exercises can enhance your ability to evaluate news sources. Ask questions about the origin of the information, the evidence supporting it, and the source's credibility. Consider whether the story aligns with facts or seems designed to provoke an emotional response.

Media literacy initiatives are also crucial in this fight. These programs teach people to critically analyze media content, recognize bias, and verify information before sharing it. By improving media literacy, you can become more discerning consumers of information and better equipped to navigate the complex media landscape. Tools like the CRAAP test (Currency, Relevance, Authority, Accuracy, and Purpose) can help you assess the reliability of sources. This framework encourages you to consider various aspects of the information you encounter, ensuring a comprehensive evaluation.

Expanding Media Literacy: Combating the Spread of Misinformation

As conspiracy theories continue to increase through modern media channels, the importance of media literacy becomes more urgent. Media literacy programs aim to equip individuals with the critical thinking skills to evaluate the information they consume, helping them distinguish between credible sources and misinformation. These initiatives focus on understanding how media operates, recognizing bias, and developing the tools to question content before accepting it as truth.

Several real-world campaigns have emerged to combat misinformation and foster media literacy. For instance, the *News Literacy Project*, a U.S.-based nonprofit, offers resources for students and the general public to sharpen their ability to identify false or misleading news. Their "Checkology" virtual classroom teaches users how to navigate the modern media landscape by dissecting news stories, identifying reliable sources, and understanding the motivations behind the content they encounter. This type of education encourages individuals to pause before sharing information and think critically about its origins and purpose.

In Europe, the European Union's *European Media Literacy Week* brings together educators, policymakers, and tech companies to highlight the importance of media literacy in the digital age. The event emphasizes the need for collaboration between governments and social media platforms to promote accurate information and teach individuals to spot fake news. Efforts like these are crucial in creating a society better equipped to resist the lure of sensational conspiracy theories and responsibly engage with news and media content.

Tools like the CRAAP test have also become popular in teaching individuals how to assess the reliability of sources. This framework encourages people to ask questions about the information they come across, evaluating whether it comes from a reputable source, is current, and aligns with factual evidence. The rise of fact-checking websites, like *Snopes* and *FactCheck.org*, also plays a significant role in the fight against misinformation, offering readers a quick way to verify the truth behind viral claims.

However, media literacy is not just about teaching people how to consume information; it's also about instilling a healthy skepticism and a commitment to seeking multiple perspectives. In a world where misinformation can spread at the speed of a click, the ability to think critically and evaluate the credibility of sources is perhaps the most powerful tool in combatting the viral spread of conspiracy theories. Expanding media literacy efforts remains essential as a long-term solution to the challenges posed by misinformation in the modern media landscape.

Understanding the mechanisms behind disinformation and fake news and adopting effective strategies to counter them is vital in today's information-saturated world. By staying informed and developing critical thinking skills, you can protect yourself from falling victim to false narratives and contribute to a more informed and rational public discourse.

In this web of deceit, the media is more than just an observer—it plays an active role in shaping narratives, often with selective reporting, intentional omissions, and sometimes outright misinformation. This pattern of suppression and distortion turns the media into a tool for those with power, amplifying certain agendas while burying inconvenient truths. For those who believe in the hidden machinations of elites, the media is no longer a trustworthy source but a key player in perpetuating these cover-ups, encouraging people to question what they're told and seek truth independently. As you continue looking for truth in the sea of available information, trust no one who hasn't earned it.

Your Review Matters: Help Spread the Curiosity of Conspiracies

"The truth will set you free, but first it will make you miserable."
– James A. Garfield

Thank you for diving into the world of conspiracy theories with me! I hope this book has been as exciting for you to read as it was for me to write. Now, I have a small favor to ask.

Imagine helping another curious mind eager to uncover the truth, just like you were. They're looking for eye-opening insights and deep dives into hidden mysteries, and your review could be the beacon that guides them.

Here's how you can make a big difference:
Please take a moment to leave a review for this book. It's quick, it's free, and it can help someone else discover the thrill of conspiracy theories. Your review could inspire:

- One more truth-seeker to question everything.

- One more reader to dive into hidden secrets with confidence.

- One more enthusiast to sharpen their understanding of the unknown.

- One more curious mind to explore the untold stories behind world events.

- One more dream of uncovering hidden truths to become a reality.

Ready to share your thoughts?
Simply click or scan the QR code below to leave your review on Amazon. It only takes a minute, but your impact could open minds for a lifetime.

CHAPTER 8

HISTORICAL CONSPIRACIES REVISITED

IMAGINE A WORLD WHERE every whispered conversation in a smoky backroom, every clandestine meeting in a dimly lit alley, could shape the destiny of nations. This was the reality of the Cold War, a time when espionage and deception were not just the stuff of spy novels but the daily bread of global superpowers. As the Iron Curtain descended across Europe, splitting it into East and West, the stage was set for one of modern history's most intense and prolonged geopolitical struggles.

The Cold War: Espionage and Deception

The Cold War was marked by a stark division between the United States and the Soviet Union, both ideologically and physically. The Iron Curtain symbolized this divide, with Eastern Europe falling under Soviet influence and Western Europe aligning with the United States and its allies. This division was not just a matter of borders but a battle of ideologies: communism versus capitalism, totalitarianism versus democracy. The Berlin Wall, constructed in 1961, became the most tangible representation of this divide, splitting Berlin into two separate entities and serving as a constant reminder of the Cold War's stakes.

At the heart of the Cold War was the nuclear arms race, a terrifying escalation of weaponry that brought the world to the brink of destruction. Both the USA and USSR amassed vast arsenals of nuclear weapons, subscribing to the doctrine of Mutual Assured Destruction (MAD). This doctrine posited that any nuclear attack by one superpower would result in a devastating retaliatory strike, ensuring the destruction of both. The Cuban Missile Crisis of 1962 brought this concept into stark relief. When the Soviet Union placed nuclear missiles in Cuba, just 90 miles from the U.S. coast, the world held its breath as the two superpowers teetered on the edge of nuclear war. President Kennedy and Premier

Khrushchev eventually reached a tense agreement, averting disaster but leaving a lasting legacy of fear and mistrust.

Espionage became a crucial tool in this high-stakes game. The period saw numerous high-profile espionage cases that significantly impacted both sides. The Cambridge Five, a ring of British spies who worked for the KGB, infiltrated the highest levels of British intelligence. Members like Kim Philby and Donald Maclean passed critical information to the Soviet Union, compromising Western operations and altering the balance of power. Their actions not only damaged British intelligence but also sowed seeds of suspicion and paranoia within Western governments.

In the United States, the case of Julius and Ethel Rosenberg shook the nation. Convicted of passing atomic secrets to the USSR, the Rosenbergs were executed in 1953, becoming the only Americans to be executed for espionage during the Cold War. Their trial and subsequent execution were highly controversial, raising questions about the fairness of their trial and the extent of their guilt. The Rosenberg case underscored the pervasive fear of communist infiltration and the lengths to which the U.S. government would go to root out perceived threats.

Another significant event was the U-2 incident in 1960. An American U-2 spy plane, piloted by Francis Gary Powers, was shot down over Soviet airspace. Powers was captured, and the incident led to a major diplomatic crisis. The U.S. initially denied the true nature of the mission, but the Soviet Union presented evidence of espionage, embarrassing the U.S. and intensifying Cold War tensions. Powers was eventually exchanged for a captured Soviet spy, but the incident highlighted the risks and consequences of espionage during this volatile period.

The Cold War also led to numerous conspiracy theories, many of which persist. Some theories claim that the Soviet Union infiltrated the U.S. government and military, placing agents in key positions to influence policy. While the existence of spies like the Rosenbergs and the Cambridge Five lends some credence to these claims, the extent of Soviet infiltration remains a topic of debate. Other theories focus on alleged secret CIA operations, including mind control experiments under programs like MKUltra, which is now known to be true. This fact and other theories suggest that the CIA conducted covert operations not only abroad but also within the United States, experimenting on citizens without their knowledge or consent.

False-flag operations are another area rife with conspiracy theories. These covert operations are designed to deceive, making it appear that other entities carried them out. Some theories allege that the U.S. conducted false-flag operations to justify military actions or political decisions. These theories gain more traction when events are proven true. For example, Operation Northwoods, a proposed plan to stage attacks on American soil and blame them on Cuba, was never executed but has fueled speculation about other false-flag operations during the Cold War.

To evaluate the credibility of these theories, it's essential to examine the available evidence critically. Declassified documents from both the U.S. and the USSR provide valuable insights into the operations and intentions of both superpowers. These documents, however, often raise as many questions as they answer, with significant portions redacted or incomplete. Testimonies from former spies and intelligence officers offer firsthand accounts, which can be biased or incomplete. Academic studies and historical analyses can help contextualize these events, providing a more comprehensive understanding of the Cold War's complexities.

Grounded in Deception

Cold War conspiracy theories are more than mere speculation—they are rooted in undeniable facts that reveal the covert and sinister actions of governments during this era. The Cold War was a period defined by secrecy, deception, and manipulation, where intelligence agencies and elites orchestrated events behind the scenes, away from public scrutiny. These *theories* have persisted because they are built on a foundation of documented government actions that confirm the lengths to which those in power will go to maintain control.

The reality is clear: both the U.S. and Soviet governments engaged in covert operations without public consent, often manipulating events to serve their own hidden agendas. Programs like the CIA's MKUltra are not just footnotes in history—they are proof of the government's willingness to exploit its own people in the name of power. These revelations aren't just confirmations of conspiracy theories—they are facts that expose the true nature of government operations during the Cold War. The secrecy that surrounded these activities fostered an environment where anything seemed possible, and much of it was true.

A Culture of Mistrust and Manipulation

Psychologically, Cold War conspiracy theories struck a nerve because they offered clarity in a world clouded by government lies and cover-ups. The looming threat of nuclear war was used as a smokescreen for covert deals, secret operations, and hidden agendas. Rather than accepting the surface narrative, many saw through the facade, recognizing that power was being wielded not by elected officials, but by shadowy elites manipulating events from behind the scenes. This was not speculation—it was the reality of Cold War politics.

The paranoia of the era wasn't unfounded. The exposure of espionage networks like the Rosenbergs and the Cambridge Five was proof that covert influence was not only real but pervasive. These espionage cases demonstrated that no one—neither governments nor their citizens—was beyond manipulation. The infiltration of governments by spies and operatives only reinforced the idea that the Cold War was a battle fought in the shadows, where the real power brokers operated beyond the reach of public accountability.

The Ongoing Influence of Cold War Conspiracies
Even today, with many Cold War secrets declassified, the true extent of covert operations remains hidden. Redacted documents and incomplete files ensure that the full story is never revealed, leaving room for further speculation. But this isn't baseless speculation—it's an acknowledgment that much of what we know is deliberately obscured. The fact that so many details remain hidden only strengthens the belief that Cold War conspiracy theories are grounded in truth.

Hollywood and the media have continued to shape the narrative, but beneath the romanticized stories of spies and intrigue lies a deeper truth: the Cold War was a time of mass deception, and its legacy continues to influence global politics. These conspiracy theories endure not because of paranoia but because they reveal the lengths governments will go to maintain control. The persistence of these theories speaks to the ongoing mistrust in government institutions, born out of the well-documented covert actions of the Cold War era.

Revelations That Confirm What Theorists Knew All Along
The declassification of projects like MKUltra and the Venona Project has only validated what conspiracy theorists long suspected: governments were engaged in secret, manipulative operations on a massive scale. The Venona Project, a U.S. counterintelligence program, uncovered extensive Soviet infiltration within American institutions, from government agencies to academic circles. This program decrypted Soviet communications, revealing a network of spies embedded in key positions across the United States. These revelations underscored the prevalence of espionage, a threat that many had dismissed or underestimated for years.

These revelations are only scratching the surface, and as more documents are declassified, it becomes clear that the full extent of Cold War deception is far greater than the public has been led to believe. Every new piece of evidence reinforces the idea that the Cold War was not just a battle between superpowers, but a series of covert operations designed to manipulate and control global events.

The Death of Princess Diana: Accident or Assassination?

On the night of August 31, 1997, the world was rocked by the tragic news that Princess Diana had been involved in a fatal car crash in the Pont de l'Alma tunnel in Paris. Diana, her companion Dodi Fayed, and driver Henri Paul were leaving the Ritz Hotel, reportedly pursued by aggressive paparazzi on motorcycles. As the car entered the tunnel, it struck a concrete pillar, leading to a catastrophic crash. Emergency services arrived promptly, but it took nearly an hour to extricate Diana from the wreckage. Despite efforts to save her, she succumbed to her injuries shortly after being admitted to the hospital, leaving millions in shock and mourning.

In the aftermath of the accident, French authorities initiated a comprehensive investigation. The preliminary findings pointed to driver error, primarily due to Henri Paul's intoxication and the reckless pursuit by photographers. Toxicology reports revealed that Paul had a blood alcohol level three times the legal limit, which, combined with high speeds, created a perilous situation. The British Metropolitan Police also conducted their inquiry, known as Operation Paget, which largely corroborated the French conclusions.

Despite the thorough investigations, conspiracy theories began to proliferate almost immediately. While the official narrative concluded that Diana's death was a tragic accident, various theories emerged suggesting that her demise was orchestrated by powerful forces. One of the most persistent theories claims that the British royal family or intelligence services arranged the crash to prevent Diana from marrying Dodi Fayed, which would have been seen as unacceptable by the establishment.

The evidence supporting the official narrative has faced intense scrutiny. The toxicology reports that highlighted Paul's impairment were central to the investigation. However, conspiracy theorists argue that these results were manipulated to shift blame solely onto Paul. They raise questions about his reputed professionalism and why he would have driven in such a state.

Trevor Rees-Jones, the bodyguard who survived the crash, provided crucial testimony supporting the official findings. Although he sustained significant injuries and had limited memory of the event, his account indicated that Paul was driving at high speed to evade the paparazzi. Critics of the official narrative suggest that investigators may have filled in the gaps in his memory to fit their conclusions.

CCTV footage from the Ritz Hotel and surrounding areas played a role in establishing a timeline of events leading to the crash. However, the absence of footage from within the tunnel itself has become a focal point for speculation. Some argue that this missing footage indicates a cover-up, while others suggest it simply reflects the technical limitations of surveillance at the time.

The cultural impact of Princess Diana's death was immense, as media coverage was relentless. Every detail of her life and tragic end was scrutinized, and public mourning was profound. The intense media scrutiny only fueled the rumors as inconsistencies and unexplained details became magnified.

Diana's legacy endures in popular culture, with films, documentaries, and books exploring various aspects of her life and the circumstances of her death. These works often present alternative possibilities, adding layers to the public's understanding and keeping the debate alive. Each anniversary of her death brings renewed interest and conjecture, reflecting her lasting impact on the collective imagination.

The Truth They Don't Want You to Know
The conspiracy surrounding Princess Diana's death is not based on a simple theory—it's often regarded as a hidden fact that powerful forces conspired to silence her. Diana herself shared in interviews before her tragic death that she feared figures within the British establishment, including Prince Philip and Prince Charles, were involved in a plan to endanger her life. She revealed that her life had been threatened by the royal family, which could make her sudden, violent death in Paris no accident—but an assassination.

The reason this *theory* persists is simple: the official narrative of a tragic car accident is a cover-up. Diana had become a thorn in the side of the monarchy, exposing its darkest secrets and threatening the very fabric of their control. She was not just "The People's Princess"; she was a woman who had defied the rigid traditions of the British royal family, and that made her a target. To those in power, Diana was dangerous, and her death was a way to silence her once and for all.

Undeniable Evidence of a Murder Plot

There is overwhelming evidence that Diana's death was no accident, although it is hard to prove with the government suppressing information. The absence of CCTV footage from the tunnel where the crash occurred, allegations of tampered evidence, and the suspicious behavior of those closest to the royal family all point to a well-executed murder plot. The narrative of an "accident" serves only to protect the royal family, who feared Diana's influence and popularity. Her death was orchestrated to preserve the monarchy's control, ensuring that her revelations never saw the light of day.

Diana's own letters serve as some of the most compelling proof. In them, she expressed her fear that she would be killed in a staged accident. She knew her life was in danger, and her fears were realized when the royal family finally had enough of her exposing their secrets. It very well could be that Diana was silenced to prevent her from revealing the full extent of their corruption and control.

The Royal Family's Role in the Cover-Up

The royal family's aloof and cold response to Diana's death only further fuels the speculation. Their behavior after her death was one of calculated indifference, as if they were relieved that the problem had been "solved." Prince Philip and Prince Charles, in particular, had much to gain from Diana's death. Her relationship with Dodi Fayed, a Muslim man, threatened to destabilize the royal family's carefully maintained image, and her increasing willingness to speak out against the institution endangered their hold on the public.

The fact that no one within the British establishment was ever held accountable for anything related to her death only reinforces the idea that this was a meticulously planned operation. The British government and intelligence agencies played their part in covering up the truth, as they have for years, ensuring that the royal family remained untouchable.

Mistrust of Institutions and Government Complicity

The British public, along with millions around the world, know the truth: governments and powerful elites will go to great lengths to protect themselves, even if it means killing someone as beloved as Princess Diana. Diana's death fits into a broader pattern of secret operations designed to protect the interests of the elite at the expense of ordinary people. The fact that these institutions—whether royal or governmental—could be involved in such a heinous act is not surprising. History has shown time and again that the powerful will do whatever is necessary to maintain control.

From Project Sunshine to the multitude of other exposed covert operations, governments have always engaged in secretive, unethical practices, and the British establishment is no different. They had the means, motive, and opportunity to orchestrate Diana's death, and the fact that the official narrative continues to ignore these potential revelations only adds fuel to the argument supporting the cover-up.

A Legacy of Truth-Telling and Continued Revelations

Theories about Diana's murder continue to gain traction not because of speculation, but because of the mounting evidence that supports them. New revelations, documentaries, and investigations continually breathe life into the fact that some of the public already think: Princess Diana was murdered because she threatened the power and influence of the British establishment. Each anniversary of her death and every new piece of information that emerges only strengthens this belief.

Diana's story should be told as one of betrayal by those who were meant to protect her. Her death, far from being a tragic accident, is remembered by many as a calculated move to safeguard the royal family's image and to prevent the full exposure of their alleged corruption.

The Case Remains Open

As more people question the official narrative, it becomes undeniably clear that the full story behind Diana's death remains hidden. To those of us who see past the façade, the truth of what happened in that Paris tunnel is known by those who orchestrated her murder—it's only a matter of time before more evidence comes to light. Diana's death is a haunting reminder of how far the powerful will go to protect their secrets, and it's our duty to expose these truths.

The Pearl Harbor Attack: Foreknowledge or Surprise?

In the early morning hours of December 7, 1941, the United States naval base at Pearl Harbor, Hawaii, stood as the principal American military installation in the Pacific. The sprawling facility, home to the U.S. Pacific Fleet, operated much like any other American military base on that Sunday morning, with routine patrols and standard peacetime protocols in effect. What unfolded in the next few hours would transform both the base and the nation, marking one of the most significant moments in American history.

The attack occurred within the broader context of escalating Pacific tensions. Throughout the late 1930s, Japan had pursued an aggressive policy of expansion across Asia, leading to increasing friction with Western powers. The United States responded with economic pressures, including a critical oil embargo and asset freeze in July 1941, measures designed to curtail Japanese military activities in China and Southeast Asia.

At 7:55 AM Hawaii time, the first wave of Japanese aircraft appeared over Pearl Harbor. The strike force, having sailed in complete secrecy across the Pacific, consisted of six aircraft carriers launching 353 aircraft in two precisely coordinated waves. The attack targeted the heart of American naval power in the Pacific—the battleships moored at Pearl Harbor's shallow-water berths.

The military consequences were severe and immediate. In less than two hours, the Japanese attack claimed 2,403 American lives and wounded 1,178 others. Eight U.S. Navy battleships suffered significant damage, with four sunk. The attack also destroyed or damaged 347 aircraft, the majority caught on the ground. The USS Arizona's destruction, which claimed 1,177 lives when a bomb detonated its forward ammunition magazine, became a powerful symbol of the attack's devastation.

The success of the Japanese strike stemmed from meticulous planning and execution. The attack force, commanded by Admiral Nagumo, maintained strict radio silence during its approach. The Japanese pilots benefited from extensive training and detailed intelligence about the harbor's layout and defensive capabilities. The timing—early Sunday morning—caught many American personnel off duty, further compromising the base's defensive readiness.

President Franklin D. Roosevelt's response was swift. The next day, December 8, he addressed Congress, delivering his famous "Day of Infamy" speech. Congress declared war on Japan with only one dissenting vote, officially bringing the United States into World War II. When Germany and Italy declared war on the United States three days later, the American entry into the global conflict was complete.

The aftermath brought immediate changes to American military operations. The Navy rapidly shifted its strategic focus from battleships to aircraft carriers—a transformation that would prove decisive in the Pacific War. Military intelligence underwent comprehensive reforms, leading to enhanced surveillance and analysis capabilities. The entire American military establishment restructured itself for total war mobilization.

The attack's impact extended far beyond military spheres. American society transformed virtually overnight from a peacetime footing to full wartime mobilization. Industries converted to military production, rationing became commonplace, and millions of

Americans volunteered for military service or war-related civilian work. The nation's isolationist sentiments, previously strong, gave way to a new understanding of America's role in global affairs.

Unveiling Pearl Harbor Foreknowledge

Now that you know what the globalists want you to believe, let's talk about how U.S. officials had prior knowledge of the Pearl Harbor attack and allowed it to happen. This *"theory"* continues to capture the public's imagination decades later. It persists for various psychological, cultural, and historical reasons that resonate with those who distrust government actions or view history through a lens of skepticism.

At its core, the alternate story appeals to a fundamental discomfort with the idea that a military superpower like the United States could have been caught so completely off guard by such a devastating attack. For some, it seems more plausible that the attack was part of a larger, hidden strategy orchestrated to sway public opinion and bring the U.S. into World War II. While I firmly believe there is convincing evidence to support this alternative narrative, I want to discuss this particular case from the perspective of answering another question: why do so many, for so long, believe the unofficial account and continue searching for the truth?

One key factor in this theory's longevity is how it taps into a broader pattern of skepticism toward government narratives. Over the years, revelations about covert operations, intelligence failures, and outright government deceit—such as Watergate and the Vietnam War—have contributed to a general mistrust in official accounts. The Pearl Harbor conspiracy fits into this larger context, where people question whether governments might allow or even orchestrate crises to serve a greater political agenda. The historical reality that President Roosevelt faced significant opposition to entering the war only strengthens the belief that the attack was a convenient pretext to unite the public and overcome isolationist sentiment.

The psychological need to make sense of tragic, large-scale events also plays a role in why this theory has endured. The loss of over 2,400 American lives and the seemingly avoidable devastation at Pearl Harbor make the official explanation—an unanticipated attack—difficult for some to accept. People tend to seek deeper, more sinister reasons for such catastrophic events, believing that something as monumental as the U.S. entry into World War II couldn't have been triggered by sheer miscalculation or negligence. Conspiracy theories offer a more structured narrative that attributes blame to hidden forces rather than randomness or incompetence. This tendency to seek more dramatic explanations for major historical events helps sustain the Pearl Harbor foreknowledge theory.

Culturally, the Pearl Harbor conspiracy endures partly because of the ongoing public fascination with World War II. The conflict remains a central part of American identity and collective memory, symbolizing both national heroism and the triumph of democracy over tyranny. Yet, within this narrative, the shock of Pearl Harbor—America's vulnerability—remains an unresolved emotional wound. The theory that the U.S. government might have allowed the attack adds complexity to a story otherwise framed by patriotism and sacrifice, creating tension between the glorified war effort and the darker suspicions of governmental manipulation.

Moreover, official investigations into Pearl Harbor, such as the Roberts Commission, have been scrutinized and challenged over the years, keeping the theory alive. The ongoing debate among historians about intelligence failures, miscommunications, and the extent of Roosevelt's knowledge leaves enough ambiguity to fuel speculation. When combined with declassified documents that reveal bits of previously hidden information, it becomes easy for theorists to point to gaps in the narrative as evidence of a larger cover-up.

In recent years, the rise of digital media and alternative news sources has further contributed to the speculation. Online forums, blogs, and documentaries continue to circulate new interpretations of the Pearl Harbor attack, offering platforms for those who reject the official narrative. As a result, each new generation can encounter and engage with the conspiracy, keeping it relevant and alive in the public consciousness.

Ultimately, the Pearl Harbor foreknowledge theory endures because it appeals to deep-seated human instincts to question authority, search for hidden motives, and seek order in the face of historical chaos. Whether rooted in fact or fueled by mistrust, the theory remains a compelling lens through which many view one of the most significant events in American history.

New Evidence and Interpretations of Foreknowledge

Now that we have discussed the why, let's discuss the what. U.S. officials having foreknowledge of the Pearl Harbor attack isn't just a speculative idea—it's a potential reality that gains more traction with each new piece of uncovered evidence. The release of declassified Magic intercepts—Japanese military communications decoded before the attack—paints a clear picture of government complicity. While these messages didn't explicitly state Pearl Harbor as the target, they pointed to heightened military activity, and the fact that U.S. officials did nothing with this intelligence seems to be no accident. This wasn't mere negligence; to many, it was a calculated decision to let the attack happen, a decision made to manipulate the American public into supporting a war that they previously resisted. A theme seen over and over in American history.

For those who look deeper, the signs of foreknowledge are undeniable. Historians have taken another look at the Roberts Commission and other so-called "inquiries" into Pearl Harbor, raising serious questions about whether these *investigations* were designed to expose the truth or merely serve as damage control. Was this an intelligence failure, or a cold, strategic move to provoke the kind of public outrage that would guarantee U.S. entry into World War II? The ongoing re-examination of this event by theorists and historians alike suggests that the truth lies in the latter.

The rise of digital media, investigative documentaries, and independent researchers has given this viewpoint new life. Despite the government's attempts to bury these inconvenient truths, modern audiences are waking up to the possibility that Pearl Harbor was no surprise attack. The steady release of declassified documents, each shedding more light on what officials knew and when, only adds fuel to the fire. These revelations, far from closing the case, have opened more doors and strengthened the belief that the U.S. government allowed Pearl Harbor to happen in order to justify war.

As we reflect on these historical events, it becomes crystal clear that the official story of Pearl Harbor could have been crafted to protect those in power. The shadows of government operations, redacted documents, and withheld truths continue to stir up unanswered questions. For those willing to challenge the mainstream narrative, the Pearl Harbor foreknowledge theory isn't a stretch—it's a necessary explanation for the tragic events that led to America's entry into World War II. The lies, the cover-ups, and the manipulation of public trust have left an indelible mark on the public consciousness, ensuring that the theory endures.

In the next chapter, we turn our attention to the global economy, where financial institutions and hidden power structures continue to shape world events, driven by the same kind of behind-the-scenes manipulation that makes Pearl Harbor a prime example of government deceit.

CHAPTER 9

ECONOMIC CONSPIRACIES AND FINANCIAL MANIPULATION

IN THE WAKE OF the 2008 financial crisis, many Americans questioned the institutions that had long been pillars of the economy. The Federal Reserve, the central banking system of the United States, became a focal point for suspicion and intrigue. Whether a seasoned economist or someone just beginning to explore the complexities of our financial system, understanding the role and purpose of the Federal Reserve is crucial for grasping the broader economic landscape.

The Federal Reserve: Control of the Economy?

The Federal Reserve, often referred to simply as "the Fed," was established in 1913 in response to a series of financial panics that highlighted the need for a central banking system. Its primary functions include regulating monetary policy, acting as a lender of last resort, and maintaining financial stability. By adjusting and controlling the money supply, the Fed promotes maximum employment, stable prices, and moderate long-term interest rates. It also supervises and regulates banks to ensure the safety and soundness of the nation's banking and financial system.

At its core, the Fed is responsible for setting the federal funds rate, which is the interest rate banks lend to each other overnight. This rate influences other interest rates, including those for mortgages, car loans, and business investments. The Fed can either cool down an overheating economy or stimulate a sluggish one by raising or lowering the federal funds rate. Additionally, the Fed is a lender of last resort, providing liquidity to banks during financial stress to prevent bank runs and maintain public confidence in the financial system. Another critical function is the supervision and regulation of banks. By conducting regular examinations and monitoring the financial health of these institutions, the Fed aims to prevent banking crises that could have severe economic repercussions.

Despite its crucial role, the Federal Reserve is often the subject of conspiracy theories that claim it has hidden agendas. One of the most persistent theories is that the Fed is privately owned and operates for the benefit of a small elite. Critics argue that the Fed's structure, with its regional and private member banks, creates a system where private interests can dominate public policy. This theory gained traction because the Federal Reserve was conceived during a secret meeting at Jekyll Island in 1910, where a group of bankers and politicians drafted the plan that would eventually lead to its creation. The secrecy surrounding this meeting has fueled suspicions of a hidden agenda ever since.

Another common allegation is that the Fed manipulates the economy to control political outcomes. Critics claim that the Fed can influence elections and policy decisions by adjusting interest rates and controlling the money supply. For example, some argue that lowering interest rates before an election can stimulate economic growth, making the incumbent administration look more favorable. Conversely, raising rates can slow down the economy, potentially harming the political prospects of those in power. These actions could suggest a level of manipulation that undermines the democratic process and places immense power in the hands of unelected officials.

Some go further and blame the Federal Reserve for causing economic recessions. They argue that the Fed's actions, whether through monetary tightening or excessive money printing, have led to financial bubbles and subsequent crashes. The 2008 financial crisis is often cited as an example, with critics claiming that the Fed's low-interest-rate policies in the early 2000s contributed to the housing bubble that eventually burst. These theories suggest that the Fed's interventions, rather than stabilizing the economy, have made it more volatile and prone to severe downturns.

Social and Cultural Context: The Erosion of Trust
Conspiracy theories resonate deeply with segments of the public because they expose the unsettling realities of power, transparency, and control. In an era marked by widening economic inequality and a palpable distrust of institutions, the belief that an unelected elite wields disproportionate control over the economy transcends mere speculation—it morphs into an urgent call for truth. The Federal Reserve's notorious opacity in shaping the financial landscape fuels skepticism, especially among those who feel cast aside by a system that serves only a select few.

Movements like Occupy Wall Street, which erupted after the 2008 financial crisis, spotlight this deep-seated mistrust. Protesters did not just raise concerns; they exposed a stark reality—the concentration of wealth and power among a handful of financial institutions.

Many of these entities profited from bailouts while ordinary Americans lost their homes and livelihoods. This glaring injustice not only ignited outrage but also gave rise to powerful conspiracy theories about the true motives behind the central banking system.

The Federal Reserve: Unmasking the Truth

Let's cut through the noise: the Federal Reserve's ownership structure is a convoluted web of public and private interests, a system that obscures the real dynamics at play. While member banks technically own the regional Federal Reserve Banks, the Board of Governors acts as a federal agency, further blurring the lines of accountability. This complexity doesn't foster trust; it invites suspicion and speculation about whose interests are truly being served.

The claim that the Fed manipulates the economy for political outcomes is not just a theory—it's a legitimate concern. The Fed's decisions often align with the interests of the powerful, and history shows us that these choices can lead to devastating consequences for the average citizen. The belief that the Fed operates independently is naive at best; it's crucial to question who truly benefits from its policies.

Conspiracy Theories and Public Trust

The implications of shady Federal Reserve actions extend far beyond mere speculation. They erode public trust and fuel movements calling for radical reform or outright abolition of central banking. Groups advocating for a return to the gold standard aren't just voicing dissatisfaction; they are rallying against a system perceived as corrupt and oppressive. Furthermore, many point to the fact that the Federal Reserve is a market manipulator, placing the free market principles that should dominate interest rates into the hands of a powerful few. For a country that touts economic freedom and free market capitalism throughout the world, involving themselves at this high level of manipulation is reckless at best.

Public confidence in central banking is fragile, and conspiracy theories thrive in this environment of uncertainty. These narratives exploit societal fears about concentrated power and financial instability, blossoming in moments of crisis—like the 2008 recession—when the actions of powerful institutions seem to favor the elite while the common person bears the brunt of economic policies.

Examples from Other Countries

The United States is not alone in grappling with these unsettling truths. The European Central Bank (ECB) has also been at the center of conspiracy theories, particularly during the Eurozone debt crisis. Critics alleged that the ECB's austerity measures disproportion-ately harmed weaker economies while benefiting stronger ones, further fueling suspicions of elite manipulation.

In volatile economies like Venezuela and Argentina, citizens point fingers at central banks for hyperinflation and economic collapse. This reality breeds deep mistrust of domestic financial institutions and the global monetary system, reinforcing the notion that these entities serve only the interests of the wealthy elite.

Unveiling the Reality

Understanding the Federal Reserve's role and the conspiracy theories surrounding it is essential for navigating the labyrinth of economic policy and financial manipulation. It's time to recognize the hidden truths that shape our economic reality. These theories are not merely idle chatter; they reflect genuine fears and frustrations that demand attention. As you explore these narratives, equip yourself with the critical thinking skills necessary to discern fact from fiction in today's media landscape.

The intricacies of the Fed's operations and the swirling theories around it compel us to question and investigate. The challenge lies in staying vigilant, recognizing the hidden forces at play, and demanding accountability from those who hold power. Unraveling these truths is just the beginning of a deeper exploration into the mechanisms that govern our lives.

The 2008 Financial Crisis: Planned or Accidental?

In the years leading up to 2008, the U.S. housing market was a bubble waiting to burst. The seeds of this crisis were sown in the late 1990s when home prices began to rise rapidly. By 2006, residential construction was booming, and homeownership was at an all-time high. Banks and financial institutions, driven by the promise of high returns, began offering subprime mortgages to borrowers with poor credit histories. These risky loans were bundled into mortgage-backed securities and sold to investors worldwide.

As home prices continued to soar, more people took out mortgages they couldn't afford, betting on the market's perpetual rise. This unsustainable growth was underpinned by low interest rates, lax lending standards, and the proliferation of complex financial prod-ucts that few truly understood. By 2007, the cracks began to show. Mortgage defaults started to rise, and the value of mortgage-backed securities plummeted. Major financial institutions, deeply invested in these toxic assets, found themselves in dire straits.

The collapse of Bear Stearns in March 2008 was a harbinger of the chaos to come. Once a titan of investment banking, Bear Stearns was brought to its knees by its exposure to subprime mortgages. The Federal Reserve brokered a deal for its acquisition by JPMorgan Chase, but the damage was done. Confidence in the financial system was eroding. In September 2008, Lehman Brothers, another major player on Wall Street, declared bankruptcy. This event triggered a global financial meltdown. Stock markets crashed, credit markets froze, and panic spread through the financial world.

Governments around the world scrambled to contain the crisis. In the United States, the Treasury Department and the Federal Reserve launched a series of unprecedented interventions. The Troubled Asset Relief Program (TARP) was established to purchase toxic assets from banks and provide them with much-needed capital. Despite these efforts, the economy plunged into a deep recession. Unemployment soared, and millions of Americans lost their homes to foreclosure.

The Social and Cultural Ripple Effects
The financial crisis wasn't just an economic event; it became a cultural turning point, eroding trust in long-standing institutions. Public anger and frustration were palpable, particularly toward Wall Street, large banks, and government regulators, all seen as complicit in creating and failing to prevent the disaster. For many, the crisis represented more than just a housing market collapse; it symbolized unchecked greed, irresponsible governance, and the devastating impact of corporate power.

Movements like Occupy Wall Street encapsulated this collective disillusionment in the following years. With slogans like "We are the 99%," the movement gave voice to a growing sense of inequality and a belief that the financial elites benefited at the expense of ordinary people. On the other end of the spectrum, the Tea Party emerged, championing reduced government intervention and opposing the bailouts that kept the banking sector afloat. Though ideologically different, both movements were fueled by the deep-seated suspicion that the system was rigged in favor of the few.

Conspiracy theories surrounding the 2008 crisis flourished in this atmosphere of distrust. Some claimed that financial elites had orchestrated the crisis for their gain. According to these theories, powerful bankers and investors manipulated the market to create a financial apocalypse, allowing them to buy up assets at rock-bottom prices. The timing of the crisis, just before a major U.S. election, fueled suspicions that it was a deliberate act to influence the political landscape. In the eyes of conspiracy theorists, the crisis was not a natural result of market forces but a calculated move to consolidate power and wealth in the hands of a few.

Deregulation and Capture

Many argue that regulatory capture and deliberate deregulation contributed to the crisis. The point here is that financial institutions lobbied for and received favorable regulations, allowing them to take excessive risks without adequate oversight. Repealing the Glass-Steagall Act in 1999, which had separated commercial and investment banking, is often cited as a critical factor. This deregulation and the rise of complex financial instruments like collateralized debt obligations (CDOs) created a perfect storm for financial disaster.

This wasn't just a regulatory oversight for some—it was part of a larger, coordinated effort to benefit the powerful. Critics suggest that the crisis was engineered to eliminate weaker financial institutions and concentrate power in the hands of a few dominant players. The rapid consolidation of banks and financial firms during and after the crisis lends some credence to this view. Large institutions like JPMorgan Chase and Goldman Sachs emerged stronger than ever, fueling perceptions that they had profited from the crisis while ordinary citizens bore the brunt of the fallout.

Counterarguments and the Complexity of the Crisis

It's essential to examine the evidence critically when determining the extent of corruption in financial systems. Transactions during the crisis reveal that some individuals and institutions profited from the turmoil. For instance, hedge funds that bet against the housing market made substantial gains. However, this alone does not prove a coordinated effort to engineer the crisis. The motivations behind these transactions were complex and varied, driven by greed, fear, and opportunism rather than a grand conspiracy.

Regulatory changes leading up to the crisis undeniably played a significant role. The deregulation of the financial industry allowed for greater risk-taking and the creation of opaque financial products. However, attributing the crisis solely to deregulation overlooks other contributing factors, such as global economic imbalances and the behavior of borrowers and lenders. The collapse of the housing market was a multifaceted event, and the crisis that followed resulted from a combination of missteps, systemic weaknesses, and unforeseen consequences rather than a singular, deliberate action.

Testimonies from whistleblowers and insiders provide valuable insights but often paint a partial picture. While some have exposed misconduct and unethical practices, others have defended the actions of financial institutions as misguided but not malicious. Many of those involved argue that while there were poor decisions and a lack of adequate oversight, the crisis was more the result of systemic flaws than a deliberate scheme by financial elites. The sheer complexity of the global financial system, combined with a failure to understand the risks involved in new financial products fully, created a perfect storm. In this view, the collapse was not orchestrated but a product of excessive risk-taking and inadequate regulation.

Impact on Public Trust and Global Examples
The long-term impact of the 2008 financial crisis continues to shape economic policy and public trust, both in the United States and globally. The erosion of trust in financial institutions and government regulatory bodies was profound, creating fertile ground for conspiracy theories. In other countries, the crisis also sparked suspicions. In Greece and Spain, for instance, austerity measures imposed in the wake of the crisis led to widespread protests and the rise of populist political movements. Many believed that these measures were unfairly punishing ordinary citizens for the failures of financial elites.

Iceland's response to the crisis was notably different. While many countries bailed out their banks, Iceland allowed its largest banks to fail and prosecuted several bankers. The Icelandic government's handling of the financial crisis, by holding bankers accountable, contrasts sharply with the approach taken by the U.S. and European countries. While Iceland's actions were praised, they also sparked deeper suspicions about the motives behind government bailouts elsewhere. This disparity has fueled not only skepticism but also created fertile ground for conspiracy theories to flourish, as people begin to view the lack of similar accountability in other countries as evidence of hidden agendas. For many, these suspicions transform into "conspiracy facts," where the belief in covert manipulation feels more like a reality than a theory.

In contrast, countries like China, which were less affected by the crisis, took note of the vulnerabilities in Western financial systems. China's government maintained stricter control over its banking sector and implemented significant stimulus measures to keep its economy afloat. The global ripple effects of the 2008 crisis reshaped economic policies and public perceptions of financial institutions, leading to heightened scrutiny and a greater demand for transparency.

The Lasting Legacy of Financial Conspiracy Theories
Theories about the 2008 financial crisis, whether based on fact, fear, or speculation, reflect a broader societal tendency to question authority, especially in times of crisis. The distrust

in financial institutions and government regulators remains a persistent issue, with the aftershocks of the crisis still influencing public opinion today. The Occupy Wall Street movement's slogan, "We are the 99%," encapsulated a widespread belief that the financial system is skewed to benefit a small elite at the expense of the majority.

Debates about financial stability and systemic risk remain ongoing. Critics argue that the financial system is still vulnerable to crises despite reforms like the Dodd-Frank Act. The interconnectedness of global markets and the complexity of financial instruments continue to pose persistent risks. Advocates for stronger regulation call for more robust oversight and the breakup of too-big-to-fail institutions. Meanwhile, others caution against overregulation, fearing it could stifle innovation and economic growth.

The 2008 financial crisis, whether seen as a catastrophic accident or a planned event, continues to influence the world. The theories surrounding it invite us to question the narratives presented by those in power and to seek a deeper understanding of the forces that shape our economy. One thing is clear: the government's bailout of dominant banks during a time when resources were needed by the masses reflects a deliberate prioritization of a select few over public welfare. This blatant disregard for widespread need has left a lasting mark on public trust, which remains strained today. Moving forward, the crisis highlights crucial lessons and pressing questions, underscoring the importance of vigilance in navigating the complex, often opaque world of global finance.

Bitcoin: Decentralized Currency or Government Plot?

Bitcoin, a term you've likely heard thrown around in tech circles and financial news, is more than just a buzzword. It's a groundbreaking innovation that has the potential to redefine our financial landscape. At its core, Bitcoin is a decentralized digital currency that operates on blockchain technology. Unlike traditional currencies controlled by central banks, Bitcoin is not governed by any single entity. Instead, it relies on a distributed ledger called the blockchain. This ledger is maintained by a network of computers, known as nodes, which validate and record every transaction. Each block in the chain contains a list of recent transactions; once added, it cannot be altered. This immutability ensures the integrity and transparency of the Bitcoin network.

The creation and structure of Bitcoin involve a process known as mining. Miners use powerful computers to solve complex mathematical problems, a process that validates transactions and adds new blocks to the blockchain. In return for their efforts, miners are rewarded with newly minted bitcoins. This process secures the network and controls the issuance of new bitcoins, making it a self-regulating system. Users store their bitcoins in digital wallets, which can be software-based or hardware-based. These wallets generate a pair of cryptographic keys: a public key, which is like an account number, and a private key, which is akin to a password. This combination ensures secure transactions and protects users' funds from unauthorized access.

One of the most intriguing aspects of Bitcoin is its emphasis on anonymity and security. When you make a transaction, your identity is not linked to your public key. This pseudonymity offers a degree of privacy that is hard to find in traditional financial systems. However, it's important to note that while the Bitcoin network is secure, the platforms and exchanges where you buy and sell bitcoins can be vulnerable to hacks and fraud. This duality has made Bitcoin a haven for those seeking financial privacy and a target for criminals.

Unveiling the Conspiracies Behind Bitcoin
Bitcoin, often heralded as the revolution that will liberate us from traditional finance, presents a façade that masks deeper, more unsettling truths. While it's marketed as a decentralized currency that empowers individuals, a closer inspection reveals a complex web of potential manipulations and hidden agendas that have led many hardline theorists to question its true purpose.

The Origins of Bitcoin: A Mystery Wrapped in Secrecy
At the heart of the Bitcoin narrative is the enigmatic figure of Satoshi Nakamoto, the pseudonymous creator whose identity remains shrouded in mystery. This ambiguity invites suspicion and speculation. Who is Satoshi? Could this individual—or group—be linked to government intelligence agencies or elite financial institutions? The potential for Bitcoin to serve as a tool of surveillance rather than liberation cannot be overlooked. The anonymity surrounding Nakamoto raises red flags for those skeptical of authority. Was this a calculated move to ensure that Bitcoin could never be claimed by any single entity, or is it a ruse designed to mask its origins?

The Double-Edged Sword of Anonymity
While Bitcoin promises anonymity and privacy, this aspect can be seen as a double-edged sword. Many argue that the very characteristics that make Bitcoin appealing—its decentralized nature and encryption—may actually provide the perfect cover for governments and corporations to monitor financial transactions without detection. The potential for blockchain technology to facilitate surveillance rather than eliminate it presents a disturbing paradox. In essence, the currency designed to free individuals from the clutches

of banks may simultaneously serve as a means for those very institutions to maintain control under a new guise.

The idea that Bitcoin could be co-opted by state powers is not far-fetched, especially given the history of governments leveraging technology for surveillance. The question becomes: how does a decentralized currency fit into a world where state surveillance is becoming increasingly sophisticated? The rise of cryptocurrencies may just represent a new method of financial oversight masquerading as freedom.

Bitcoin as a Tool for Elitist Control

Another angle posits that Bitcoin is not just an alternative to fiat currency, but rather a carefully orchestrated experiment by the elites to reshape the financial landscape in their favor. The 2008 financial crisis laid the groundwork for Bitcoin's emergence, creating a public thirst for an alternative to a corrupt system. However, this desperation may have played directly into the hands of those in power.

It is not far-fetched to think that Bitcoin's rapid rise could be intentionally facilitated by those who stand to gain from its adoption. By promoting Bitcoin as a revolutionary financial tool, elites can distract the masses from the real issues at hand—such as economic inequality and the concentration of wealth. This could be seen as a method of social engineering, where the allure of decentralization is used to placate public anger while the existing power structures remain intact.

Bitcoin's Role in Global Financial Instability

As Bitcoin gains traction, it's arguable that its very existence poses a threat to the stability of traditional currencies. This destabilization could be a deliberate strategy employed by elites to create chaos in the financial systems of weaker nations, allowing for greater control over the global economy. It's not a challenge to find this appealing to the globalist agenda, to say the least. The use of Bitcoin in countries like Venezuela, where citizens turn to cryptocurrency in the face of hyperinflation, has been necessary but also illustrates the potential for Bitcoin to undermine traditional financial systems.

However, this raises the question: is Bitcoin genuinely a lifeline for those in financial peril, or is it an engineered solution designed to further entrench elite interests? By presenting Bitcoin as a savior, elites could deflect blame for systemic failures while consolidating their power in a new financial paradigm.

Government Responses: Control or Coercion?

The reactions of governments to Bitcoin provide another layer of conspiracy. Countries like China have cracked down on cryptocurrency operations, fearing that Bitcoin could destabilize their economies. The narrative that governments are protecting their citizens from financial harm obscures a more sinister possibility: they may be attempting to eliminate a threat to their control. The ban on Bitcoin mining and exchanges could signify a desperate attempt to maintain power over monetary systems that are increasingly viewed as obsolete by the populace.

Moreover, the exploration of Central Bank Digital Currencies (CBDCs) represents an effort to counteract the rise of decentralized currencies. While proponents argue that CBDCs can modernize monetary systems, skeptics contend that they may merely serve to reinforce state control over financial transactions. If governments succeed in adopting their own digital currencies, they could effectively siphon off the appeal of Bitcoin while keeping citizens under surveillance.

The Future of Bitcoin: Freedom or Enslavement?

As Bitcoin evolves, its implications for the future of finance grow more significant. Advocates champion it as a beacon of financial freedom, yet the potential for it to be manipulated by those in power casts a shadow over its revolutionary promise. The fear is that as Bitcoin becomes more mainstream, it could morph from a symbol of independence into a tool of coercion.

In this context, critical thinking demands understanding Bitcoin's dual nature. Is it a genuine alternative to corrupt, centralized financial systems, or merely a façade designed to placate a restless populace while the elite globalists continue to wield control? As institutions like the Federal Reserve adapt to the changing financial landscape, the question remains whether Bitcoin will empower individuals or become yet another mechanism for oppression. It becomes essential to maintain a vigilant perspective, questioning the motives of those who promote or disparage Bitcoin. The truth lies not just in the technology itself but in the broader context of economic power struggles that shape our world.

Bitcoin's future extends beyond mere financial transactions; it represents a pivotal struggle for freedom and control within an increasingly complex financial landscape. This exploration encourages readers to stay vigilant and discerning, as only by exposing the forces at play can we uncover deeper truths about Bitcoin and the narratives shaping our understanding of modern finance.

CHAPTER 10

HEALTH AND PHARMACEUTICAL CONSPIRACIES

In 1910, a meeting took place on Jekyll Island, Georgia, involving some of the most powerful bankers and financial minds of the time. This secretive gathering laid the groundwork for what would become the Federal Reserve. The secrecy and the influential figures involved sparked countless theories about hidden agendas and control. Fast-forward to today, a similar shadow of suspicion looms over the pharmaceutical industry, often called "Big Pharma."

Big Pharma: Cures Hidden for Profit?

Big Pharma, the giant conglomerate of the pharmaceutical industry, has evolved into a powerful force that shapes global healthcare. But beneath the surface of its glossy marketing and promises of cures lies a complex web of greed, manipulation, and betrayal. While the industry has made significant advancements in medicine, the question remains: at what cost?

Big Pharma's ascent is steeped in history that many prefer to gloss over. Companies like Merck and Pfizer, once small apothecaries, transformed into titans of industry driven by a singular focus: profit. The establishment of regulatory bodies like the FDA was supposed to safeguard public health, but what has unfolded is a system where pharmaceutical executives often rotate in and out of these regulatory positions. This revolving door raises alarming questions about conflicts of interest and accountability, as those who should be regulating drug safety are, in many cases, the very individuals profiting from them.

The promise of transparency is a hollow one in a landscape dominated by corporate interests. Allegations that pharmaceutical companies hide cures to maintain profits aren't merely conspiracy theories; they resonate with a growing distrust rooted in real incidents. Take, for example, the extensive research funding for chronic disease treatments, which generates ongoing revenue streams. If cures for diseases like cancer existed, the financial implications for these companies would be catastrophic. Why would they relinquish a cash cow?

Moreover, the industry's penchant for selective reporting in clinical trials paints a bleak picture of ethics. Numerous studies have shown that pharmaceutical companies often manipulate research outcomes to highlight the efficacy of their products while down-playing adverse effects. A direct result of companies like Purdue Pharma aggressively marketing addictive painkillers while ignoring their dangers serves as a prime example of this manipulation. The fallout from such actions illustrates not only a disregard for patient safety but a deeper commitment to profit at any cost.

Big Pharma's strategies extend beyond pharmaceuticals. The suppression of alternative medicine has long been suspected, with advocates for natural remedies claiming that non-patentable treatments are systematically marginalized. This narrative of suppression invites scrutiny, especially when natural cures have shown promise but lack the financial backing of pharmaceutical giants. The truth is that treatments that can't be patented offer little incentive for a profit-driven industry to pursue them, allowing a culture of skepticism toward anything that threatens the status quo to thrive.

One of the most compelling conspiracy theories is the belief that a cure for cancer exists but is being withheld from the public. With billions poured into cancer research, the slow pace of progress leads many to wonder if a deliberate cover-up is at play. The market for cancer treatments is not just lucrative; it is colossal, generating staggering profits for companies that perpetuate the need for ongoing therapies like chemotherapy and radiation. Critics argue that this creates an environment where the focus shifts away from actual cures in favor of treatments that ensure continuous profit.

The response from governments regarding Big Pharma is equally suspect. The notion that governments prioritize public health is naive when considering the power they wield over pharmaceutical regulation. Instead of being protectors of public health, they often act as enablers, facilitating a system that allows Big Pharma to flourish unchecked. This begs the question: Are governments colluding with Big Pharma to ensure a continuous flow of profits, all while the public is led to believe they are acting in their best interest?

The fallout from these revelations is significant. Trust in healthcare and pharmaceutical companies has eroded, and conspiracy theories surrounding Big Pharma proliferate. As patients become disillusioned, they may abandon necessary treatments, opting for unproven alternatives that promise more than they can deliver. This behavior can have dire consequences, as individuals seek out remedies that are not only ineffective but potentially harmful.

Public outcry against Big Pharma has fueled demands for greater transparency and accountability. Advocacy movements pushing for healthcare transparency highlight the urgent need for reforms that ensure ethical practices within the pharmaceutical industry. A call for independent research and unbiased reporting is not merely a plea; it is a necessary condition for restoring faith in medical advancements.

As we confront the complexities of Big Pharma, we must remain vigilant in questioning the narratives presented to us. The ongoing battle between profit and public health will shape the future of our healthcare system. Understanding the intricacies of this industry is crucial, not just for our health but for the integrity of the entire healthcare system. By unveiling the motives behind Big Pharma's actions, we empower ourselves to seek genuine solutions rather than superficial remedies.

In this exploration of Big Pharma's role in our lives, I invite readers to stay alert and discerning. The interplay of power, greed, and manipulation runs deep within this industry, and only by continuing the search for truth can we hope to reclaim our health and well-being from those who prioritize profit over people.

Vaccines: Protection or Population Control?

Vaccines, once heralded as miraculous advancements in public health, now warrant a far more scrutinized examination. They represent a battle against diseases and a tool of control wielded by an industry with a long history of questionable practices. The narrative that vaccines are purely for public good obscures the dark realities behind their development and distribution.

Throughout history, vaccines have been marred by instances where the well-being of the public has taken a backseat to corporate interests. As the pharmaceutical industry expanded, it became evident that the same entities promising protection were also invested in maintaining a cycle of dependency on their products. The real question is whether these companies genuinely seek to eradicate diseases or if they benefit more from ongoing treatments that guarantee a steady income stream. It doesn't take long to see that these companies are incentivized to keep people sick and cures under wraps.

The COVID-19 pandemic has thrown this dynamic into stark relief. The rapid development and rollout of vaccines were heralded as a triumph of science, but for many, it felt like a rehearsed script in a larger play about control. This was not just about health; it was a global experiment to test obedience and compliance among populations. The enforced isolation and restrictions only fueled the fire of skepticism. Many argue that the pandemic served as a cover to initiate a mass MKUltra-like operation, desensitizing people to manipulation and control, and injecting them with substances whose true components we may never fully know.

Because of the controversial structure of executives running the regulatory bodies, questions arise about who is truly in charge of ensuring vaccine safety. When those responsible for approving vaccines also have ties to the companies profiting from them, the lines between oversight and complicity blur. This situation raises red flags, suggesting a system where accountability is sacrificed for profit.

The narrative surrounding vaccines is often one of safety and efficacy, but this portrayal can be deceptive. Those who dare to question the official story are often met with ridicule or worse—censorship. Claims that vaccines could potentially cause harm or that there are viable alternative treatments are quickly dismissed, creating an environment ripe for conspiracy theories to flourish.

The consequences of this mistrust can be severe. Vaccine hesitancy, fueled by mistrust of Big Pharma and its motives, leads to lower vaccination rates. The repercussions are evident in outbreaks of preventable diseases, where communities that once thrived on herd immunity now face the resurgence of ailments once thought eradicated. This decline in public health can often be traced back to the distrust sown by an industry more concerned with profits than safety. In the case of COVID, the opposite occurred, with people overly trusting a vaccine that later proved to not be as "safe and effective" as promised.

Looking ahead, the future of vaccines raises more questions than answers. With the advent of mRNA technology and its rapid adoption, one must wonder if this represents true progress or a new form of control. As the lines between health, surveillance, and profit continue to blur, the responsibility falls on the public to remain vigilant. Are we witnessing the evolution of healthcare, or is this merely an updated guise for the age-old battle against corporate greed?

The intricate web of Big Pharma, regulatory capture, and public health narratives is rife with manipulation and profit motives. As we peel back the layers of deception surrounding vaccines, it becomes increasingly clear that what is presented as a means of protection could very well be a sophisticated tool of control. The fight for genuine health freedoms continues, and unveiling these hidden truths is just the beginning of a necessary confrontation with the powers that be.

AIDS: A Manufactured Virus?

The origins of AIDS have been shrouded in controversy since it was first identified in the early 1980s. While mainstream narratives suggest a natural progression of a virus crossing from animals to humans, conspiracy theorists argue that AIDS is not merely a disease but a manufactured virus with deep ties to military and pharmaceutical agendas. The notion that AIDS was caused by a natural mutation is increasingly viewed with skepticism by those who explore the more disturbing possibilities surrounding its creation.

One of the most compelling theories posits that AIDS was engineered as a biological weapon, a sinister plot hatched by those in power to target specific populations. Proponents of this theory argue that the U.S. military, in its quest for biological warfare capabilities, may have inadvertently—or deliberately—created HIV in a lab. This theory gains traction when considering the government's history of unethical experimentation, including notorious programs like MKUltra. The parallels drawn between these historical atrocities and the emergence of AIDS lead many to believe that the virus's origins are not as innocent as portrayed.

As the epidemic unfolded, Big Pharma stepped into the limelight, profiting immensely from the crisis. The pharmaceutical industry has a vested interest in maintaining a constant stream of patients requiring antiretroviral drugs, which manage but do not cure HIV. Critics argue that the business model of pharmaceutical giants is predicated on treating chronic conditions rather than eradicating diseases. This raises a critical question: is the focus of AIDS now on lifelong treatment to ensure profits, rather than a genuine effort to find a cure? The sheer scale of revenue generated from treatments has led some to conclude that there's little incentive for companies to pursue a true cure, which would undermine their lucrative business.

Adding fuel to the fire, some evidence supports the notion that the AIDS epidemic is intricately linked to polio vaccine trials conducted in Africa during the mid-20th century. They argue that the virus was inadvertently introduced to humans through contaminated vaccines, a claim that resonates with those aware of historical instances of unethical medical practices targeting vulnerable populations. While mainstream science dismisses this theory, the rational fear persists, stemming from a long history of exploitation and betrayal by medical authorities.

The idea that AIDS is a manufactured virus is further complicated by the involvement of government and regulatory bodies. Many argue that agencies like the CDC and WHO operate more as protectors of corporate interests than guardians of public health. Their regulatory frameworks often favor pharmaceutical companies, creating a perception that public safety is secondary to profit. This raises an unsettling question: are these organizations merely puppets, colluding with Big Pharma to suppress information and maintain the status quo?

To discuss AIDS without addressing the theory of a government-created disease, allegedly released to target specific communities, would be leaving the story half-told. Although it is challenging to break through barriers to substantiate these claims, a strong constituency firmly believes in the government's role in the creation of AIDS. Meanwhile, others will loudly assert that AIDS originated from human interaction with apes, despite the lack of credible evidence for this narrative. Although government involvement can obscure evidence, I stand firmly with those who believe that military scientists engineered AIDS as a biochemical weapon. I'll remain in this camp until the government demonstrates genuine transparency and gives the public real reason to trust its claims about health and safety.

In conclusion, the story of AIDS is far from over. While mainstream narratives paint a picture of progress and understanding, the darker truths waiting to be unveiled challenge us to look beyond the surface. Are we witnessing a genuine public health crisis, or is it a carefully constructed façade masking the relentless pursuit of profit and control brought about by purposeful tampering? As we dig deeper into these investigations, we must remain vigilant, questioning the motives of those who wield power in the healthcare industry and demanding transparency in an era of unprecedented secrecy. The fight for truth surrounding AIDS is not just about the past; it's about the future of healthcare and the rights of individuals to seek and receive genuine care.

Fluoridation: Public Health Measure or Overreach?

Government-led public health initiatives have long been the target of suspicion and conspiracy theories, especially involving widespread, mandatory changes. One of the most prominent examples is the fluoridation of water, a practice that began in the mid-20th century in the United States and quickly spread to other countries. Health authorities champion fluoridation as a simple and effective way to prevent tooth decay, especially in communities with limited access to dental care. Yet, despite its clear benefits, the initiative has sparked enduring controversy, fueling concerns about government overreach and public manipulation.

The Origins of Fluoridation

They want you to believe that the idea of adding fluoride to drinking water emerged in the 1940s after research indicated that naturally occurring fluoride in water helped reduce the prevalence of cavities. According to the mainstream narrative, Grand Rapids, Michigan, became the first city in the U.S. to add fluoride to its public water supply in 1945, resulting in a significant reduction in tooth decay, especially among children. This led to a nationwide push for fluoridation, promoted by public health officials as a low-cost, highly effective way to improve dental health on a broad scale.

However, for those of us who question government motives, there's another angle to consider. Some claim that fluoridation's roots go back to Nazi concentration camps, where fluoride was allegedly used to keep detainees compliant and subdued. Whether or not this story holds, it casts a shadow on the official narrative. Why would such a potent substance be added to something as vital as our drinking water? And if fluoride's primary purpose is dental, why not leave it in toothpaste—where people can opt in or out as they choose? Something about this mass addition doesn't add up, and it's worth asking why.

Mistrust of Government and Science

The debate over fluoridation isn't merely about dental health—it's a conversation about the government's right to medicate the public without consent. For many who oppose fluoridation, it's seen as part of a broader pattern of state intervention in personal health decisions. The idea that fluoride is being added to water without any individual choice has transformed it into a powerful symbol for those who fear government overreach. For these people, fluoridation isn't about protecting teeth; it's about control.

And while proponents cite science, the complexity surrounding fluoride's health effects creates plenty of room for doubt. Studies show fluoride in small amounts can benefit dental health, yet high exposure levels have been linked to fluorosis, a condition leading to tooth discoloration and even bone damage in severe cases. Opponents of fluoridation point to fluorosis as evidence that the government is downplaying the risks of fluoride exposure. Proponents and opponents alike cherry-pick data, leaving the public in a sea of confusing claims, and only heightening mistrust.

The Role of Media and Pop Culture in Amplifying Mistrust

Fluoridation has a long history in the media and pop culture as well. In the 1950s and 60s, opponents often linked fluoridation to fears of communism and government control, claiming it was a tool for weakening the American public. In that era of Cold War paranoia, the fear of foreign influence made fluoridation an easy target. To this day, fluoride is sometimes referenced in film and TV as a symbol of government conspiracy, subtly feeding skepticism toward public health initiatives with mandatory or widespread reach.

The Persistence of Fluoride Conspiracy Theories

Despite decades of endorsements from health officials, fluoride conspiracy theories persist. This resilience is fueled by a broader belief that public health measures serve hidden agendas. To people already distrustful of official narratives, fluoridation is yet another example of concealed truths about what's in our water.

Today, anti-fluoridation campaigns often overlap with broader health-related conspiracy movements, including anti-vaccine advocacy and alternative health circles. These groups see fluoridation as one more instance of governments and pharmaceutical companies pushing substances onto the public for control or profit. The fluoridation debate continues as a reflection of the struggle between perceived individual rights and enforced public health measures.

The Global Debate

Fluoridation isn't just an American issue; it sparks debate worldwide. Some countries, like the U.S., Canada, and Australia, have made water fluoridation part of their public health policy, while many European countries have chosen to avoid it. These countries favor alternative methods like fluoridated salt or dental treatments, arguing that water fluoridation reduces individual choice. This difference in approach raises questions about why the U.S. insists on fluoridation if other nations see it as unnecessary.

In Europe, the decision not to fluoridate water often comes down to cultural attitudes valuing personal autonomy. Public health authorities may not reject fluoride's benefits but choose to deliver it in ways that respect individual choice. The widespread U.S. approach stands out, leading some to speculate that the emphasis on fluoridation has less to do with health and more to do with controlling the population.

Restoring Trust Through Transparency

The fluoride debate highlights a fundamental need for transparency in public health decisions. When the government mandates policies without fully explaining them, suspicion
naturally arises. In the case of fluoridation, the lack of clear communication has left room
for conspiracy theories to take hold. Trust doesn't come from unexplained mandates;
it comes from transparency, accountability, and respecting the public's right to make
informed choices.

If the government truly has public interest at heart, it would offer full transparency about
the science and motives behind fluoridation. Public health initiatives work best when they
don't just present scientific facts but also respect cultural values and individual rights.
As it stands, the fluoride debate is a small piece of a much larger problem: the growing
rift between public health authorities and a populace increasingly wary of institutional
motives.

CHAPTER 11

SECRET SOCIETIES AND HIDDEN AGENDAS

IN HISTORY'S DIMLY LIT corridors, secret societies have always captured the imagination, evoking images of clandestine meetings, hidden rituals, and powerful figures shaping the world from the shadows. One such society that has fueled countless speculations and theories is the Freemasons. To understand the allure and mystery surrounding the Freemasons, we must first trace their origins, explore their organizational structure, and examine the rituals that have fascinated and alarmed the public.

The Freemasons: Brotherhood or Shadow Government?

The roots of modern-day Freemasonry stretch back to the medieval period, originating from the guilds of stonemasons who built the cathedrals and castles of Europe. These guilds were groups of skilled laborers and craftsmen who banded together to protect their trade secrets and ensure the quality of their work. Over time, these stonemasonry guilds evolved into a more formal organization. In 1717, the Grand Lodge of England was established, marking the formal inception of modern Freemasonry. This event took place in London when four lodges came together to form a grand lodge, laying the foundation for the global network we recognize today.

As the influence of Freemasonry grew, so did its reach. Lodges began to spring up across Europe and eventually spread to other continents. By the 18th and 19th centuries, Freemasonry had established a significant presence in the Americas, Africa, and Asia. The organization's appeal lies in its emphasis on fraternity, moral development, and philanthropy. Members, known as Freemasons, were drawn from various walks of life, including influential figures in politics, business, and the arts. This global expansion fostered a network of interconnected lodges that maintained a degree of uniformity in their rituals and traditions.

Freemasonry is structured hierarchically, with members progressing through different degrees as they gain experience and knowledge. The basic organizational unit is the lodge, where members gather regularly to conduct their activities. Lodges are typically headed by a Master, supported by other officers who perform specific roles. Members begin their journey as Entered Apprentices, the first degree in Freemasonry. As they advance, they become Fellow Crafts and, ultimately, Master Masons. Each degree involves a series of rituals and teachings designed to impart moral and philosophical lessons.

The rituals and symbols of Freemasonry are shrouded in secrecy, contributing to the air of mystery surrounding the organization. Key symbols include the compass and square, which represent the tools of the stonemason and serve as metaphors for moral and ethical conduct. The all-seeing eye, another prominent symbol, signifies the omnipresence of a higher power watching over humanity. Freemasons take oaths of secrecy, pledging to protect the organization's rituals and teachings from outsiders. These oaths and the closed nature of Masonic meetings have fueled suspicions and speculations about the true intentions of the fraternity.

Conspiracy theories surrounding the Freemasons are numerous and varied, often alleging hidden agendas and undue influence over global affairs. One of the most persistent claims is that Freemasons wield significant political power and control over governments. Many argue that the organization's network of influential members enables it to manipulate political decisions and policies behind the scenes. Historical events such as the American Revolution and the French Revolution have been linked to Masonic influence, with some theorists suggesting that Freemasons played a crucial role in orchestrating these upheavals to further their goals.

Another common theory posits that the Freemasons are involved in major historical events and revolutions. Proponents of this idea point to the presence of notable Freemasons among the United States' founding fathers, including George Washington and Benjamin Franklin. They argue that Masonic principles and connections facilitated the success of the American Revolution. Similar claims have been made about the French Revolution, with theorists suggesting that Masonic lodges served as breeding grounds for revolutionary ideas and actions.

Believed by many to be the most likely is that the Freemasons are working towards establishing a New World Order. This idea suggests that the organization aims to create a single global government controlled by a select few to exert dominion over the world. Symbols associated with Freemasonry, such as the all-seeing eye on the dollar bill, are often cited as evidence of this hidden agenda. The secrecy and exclusivity of Masonic rituals and meetings indicate a broader plan to consolidate power and control.

Far beyond a brotherhood dedicated to moral and philanthropic pursuits, the Freemasons are central figures in a vast network of influence. Call it what you will—the Freemasons, the global elite, or the Deep State—but the impact of their actions reverberates in countless realms of society, from government to finance. As long as their secrets remain hidden, many will see the Freemasons as key players in an enduring agenda to reshape the world.

The Bilderberg Group: Global Elites in Control?

In the spring of 1954, a prince from the Netherlands, Prince Bernhard, laid the groundwork for what would become one of the most secretive and speculated upon gatherings in modern history: the Bilderberg Group. The initial purpose was simple yet ambitious—fostering dialogue between Europe and North America in a post-World War II landscape. This annual meeting quickly became a forum where political leaders, business executives, academics, and media moguls could discuss pressing global issues away from the public eye. The intent was to create a space for open and frank discussions, free from the constraints of official positions and the scrutiny of the press.

The exclusivity of the Bilderberg meetings is one of their most defining characteristics. These gatherings are not just invite-only; they are shrouded in strict confidentiality. The Chatham House Rule governs the discussions, allowing attendees to use the information received but not to reveal the identity or affiliation of the speakers. This rule aims to encourage open dialogue, but it also fuels suspicion. No official records, detailed agendas, resolutions, or policy statements are issued. Media coverage is minimal, and information leaks are rare, adding to the air of mystery. The small size of the meetings, typically around 130 participants, further limits public access and scrutiny.

Proponents of conspiracy theories about the Bilderberg Group argue that this secrecy is not just a matter of privacy but a cover for more sinister activities. One of the most common allegations is that the group plots global economic and political strategies. Critics claim that the attendees, who come from influential sectors of society, use the meetings to coordinate actions that serve their interests at the expense of the general public. They point to the presence of high-profile figures and the group's longevity as evidence of its significant but hidden influence.

Another prevalent theory is that the Bilderberg Group orchestrates major global events and crises. For instance, some claim that the group played a pivotal role in the 2008 financial crisis. According to this theory, the crisis was not an unfortunate accident but a deliberate manipulation to consolidate financial power and control. Proponents argue that the timing of the crisis and the subsequent bailouts benefited a select few while devastating economies worldwide. They suggest that such an elaborate scheme could only be orchestrated by a powerful and secretive organization like the Bilderberg Group.

Perhaps the most common idea is, once again, that the Bilderberg Group is working towards establishing a global government. This idea posits that the group aims to create a centralized authority that governs the world, effectively erasing national sovereignty. Symbols and phrases associated with globalization are often cited as evidence, and the group's meetings are portrayed as steps toward this ultimate goal. The secrecy and high-profile nature of the attendees lend credence to the idea that something significant, and possibly nefarious, is being planned behind closed doors. You start to see this theme over and over within secret societies—the aim to create a new global system of government, and it is not a far stretch.

The Bilderberg Group's secrecy and the high-profile influence of its attendees only strengthen suspicions that this is yet another assembly aligned with an underlying globalist agenda. Considering their closed-door meetings and the influential positions held by members—spanning finance, politics, and media—the group fits a pattern seen in other secretive organizations believed to steer global policies. Whether they acknowledge it openly or not, Bilderberg's annual gatherings are carefully choreographed moves toward a one-world government designed to consolidate control and direct the course of international events from behind the scenes. For those questioning this relentless drive toward globalization, the Bilderberg Group's presence remains a stark reminder of the shadows cast by elite power structures over national sovereignty.

Skull and Bones: The Power Behind the Power?

Skull and Bones, one of the most enigmatic and exclusive secret societies, was established in 1832 at Yale University by William Huntington Russell and Alphonso Taft. The society was born out of a desire to create a select group of individuals who would go on to wield significant influence in various sectors of society. Membership is highly exclusive, with only 15 senior students being "tapped" each year to join the ranks. Over the years, the society has produced numerous notable alumni, including three U.S. Presidents—William Howard Taft, George H. W. Bush, and George W. Bush—as well as Supreme Court justices and influential business leaders. This lineage of powerful figures has only fueled the mystique and speculation surrounding the organization.

The rituals and symbols associated with Skull and Bones are steeped in secrecy and tradition. The society's headquarters, known as the "Tomb," is a windowless building on the Yale campus that adds to the air of mystery. Initiation ceremonies are held within the Tomb and involve elaborate and macabre rites, including symbols like the skull and crossbones and the number 322. The significance of the number 322 is debated, but some suggest it refers to the death of the Greek orator Demosthenes in 322 BCE. Members take an oath of silence regarding the society's activities and rituals, ensuring that the inner workings of Skull and Bones remain largely hidden from public view. This secrecy has led to various rumors and conspiracy theories about the society's true purpose and influence.

One of the most persistent conspiracy theories about Skull and Bones is that it is a grooming ground for future leaders who will go on to control key institutions in the United States and beyond. The theory suggests that the society's members are carefully selected and trained to take on significant roles in government, finance, and other influential sectors. Proponents of this theory point to the impressive list of alumni who have achieved high-ranking positions, arguing that their success is not merely coincidental but a result of the strategic influence of Skull and Bones. The society's network is believed to provide members with unparalleled opportunities and connections, facilitating their rise to power.

Skull and Bones has long been suspected of directly influencing U.S. government policies and decisions. While the society's secrecy makes this difficult to prove outright, the paths of its members, once in power, suggest they often align on policies that seem to serve shared interests. For instance, both George H. W. Bush and George W. Bush were members of Skull and Bones, and their foreign policy and economic decisions have often been cited as reflecting this affiliation. The society's exclusivity and secrecy only reinforce this, making it challenging to disprove such patterns.

Theories about the society's connections to other secret organizations also abound. It is believed Skull and Bones is part of a larger network of secret societies working together to achieve common goals. These theories often link Skull and Bones to groups like the Freemasons and the Illuminati, suggesting that they are all part of a grand conspiracy to establish a New World Order. It is arguable that the members of these societies share a common vision of global domination and use their combined influence to steer world events in their favor. This idea is supported by the fact that many prominent figures have been associated with multiple secret societies, creating an intricate web of connections that fuels speculation.

The allure and mystery of Skull and Bones, much like other secret societies, lie in what we are left to imagine. With the society's prominent members and its tightly guarded secrets, we are expected to accept the narrative that these groups operate independently or benignly. But as we see the same patterns and connections emerging again and again, it becomes increasingly apparent that these aren't isolated entities. Call it Skull and Bones, Freemasonry, or the Deep State—these are names for a larger, coordinated agenda driven by a desire for control and power on a global scale.

Bohemian Grove: Elites, Rituals, and Secrecy in the Woods

Hidden away in the dense redwood forests of Northern California lies Bohemian Grove, a place where some of the world's most powerful men gather for an annual retreat. This secluded 2,700-acre compound, owned by the Bohemian Club, hosts a two-week event every July that has attracted U.S. presidents, corporate titans, and influential figures from various sectors. The Bohemian Club was founded in 1872 in San Francisco by journalists, artists, and musicians. Over time, however, its membership expanded to include prominent political leaders, business executives, and global influencers, transforming the club into an elite institution.

Bohemian Grove has long been a subject of fascination due to its high-profile attendees and the mystery surrounding its gatherings. The exclusive nature of the retreat, coupled with the elaborate ceremonies and rituals conducted there, has sparked numerous conspiracy theories. Critics often view Bohemian Grove as more than just a retreat, speculating that it is a space where powerful men plan and execute global agendas. Just look at the Grove's historical significance, particularly in light of some of its most notable guests, including Richard Nixon, Ronald Reagan, and Henry Kissinger.

One of the most talked-about aspects of Bohemian Grove is its signature ritual, the "Cremation of Care." This ceremony, performed at the start of the retreat, is a dramatic, theatrical event in which members gather at an outdoor amphitheater beneath a towering 40-foot stone owl—an ancient symbol of wisdom. A robed figure representing "Care" is symbolically sacrificed, signifying that attendees are freeing themselves from the burdens and responsibilities of the outside world during their stay at the Grove. The ritual is intended to help participants leave behind the stress of business and politics and engage in relaxed, informal networking. Those familiar with the retreat argue that the ceremony is simply a way for members to embrace relaxation and fellowship symbolically. But to everyone else, the ritual is just plain creepy.

The secrecy surrounding Bohemian Grove adds it to the list of numerous groups that pique curiosity. The strict no-media policy, along with a long-standing tradition of privacy, means that very little is known about what transpires within the confines of the camp. Even the members are notoriously tight-lipped about their experiences, further fueling speculation. Attendees are forbidden from discussing Grove activities with the public, and non-members are rarely granted access to the event.

This lack of transparency helps conceal the important political and business decisions during the retreat. World events, including wars, economic strategies, and presidential elections, have been shaped at Bohemian Grove. Because of the privacy and confidentiality requirements, there is no concrete evidence to support these claims. Still, it is undeniable that the gathering of such a concentration of global power in one place naturally raises questions about the nature of their conversations.

Bohemian Grove's guest list reads like a who's who of American politics, business, and entertainment. Past attendees include multiple U.S. presidents, such as Dwight D. Eisenhower, Ronald Reagan, and Richard Nixon. Corporate leaders like General Motors, Microsoft, and Boeing have also been frequent guests. The event has even attracted figures from the arts, including well-known actors and musicians. The Grove is unique in bringing together individuals from various fields, allowing them to connect and share ideas in a secluded environment free from public scrutiny.

Membership in the Bohemian Club is notoriously exclusive, and the waiting list to join can span years if not decades. While the club originally attracted individuals from the arts and literature, it now mostly consists of high-ranking political figures, corporate executives, and financiers. Many see the retreat as a way for elites to build informal networks that could later influence their fields.

Given the caliber of attendees and the mystique surrounding the event, it's no surprise that Bohemian Grove has been linked to theories about global control and the formation of shadow governments. It is easy to see the retreat is more than just a place to unwind and socialize. It is where the world's most powerful men discuss secret plans for world domination. Another organization contributing to the New World Order theory might sound redundant, but it is just one more example of this elitist global agenda under a different brand. One question that should come to mind now is whether these groups are in competition or in cahoots.

These secret organizations may indeed be implementing hidden agendas, and there could be even more elusive groups yet to be uncovered. As we scrutinize the world around us, it's important to remember that our minds are often quick to interpret ordinary events or groups as shrouded in secrecy. Just as these organizations can be perceived as operating in ways that seem mysterious or nefarious, it's equally crucial to recognize how group identity can influence the way we argue for our theories. If not careful, this influence can push even the most plausible ideas into the realm of the unbelievable. In the next chapter, we'll explore the powerful role of social dynamics and discover how to leverage them effectively—without letting groupthink or conformity dilute the strength of your arguments.

CHAPTER 12

THE SOCIAL PSYCHOLOGY OF CONSPIRACY THEORIES

CONSPIRACY THEORIES HAVE ALWAYS had a unique hold on the human mind, fueled by deep-seated cognitive biases and reinforced by social dynamics. From the allure of hidden knowledge to the comfort of tight-knit communities, believing in conspiracies taps into fundamental aspects of how we think, feel, and interact with others. This chapter explores the psychological and sociological factors that drive these beliefs, shedding light on why conspiracy theories persist, how they are shaped by group identity, and what strategies can help counter their influence. By exploring these elements, we can better understand the powerful hold conspiracy theories have on individuals and society and how we might reclaim critical thinking in the face of such complex narratives.

Social Dynamics and the Spread of Conspiracy Theories

When exploring conspiracy theories, it's easy to get swept up in group dynamics and the sense of belonging that comes with being part of a community that "knows the truth." While this sense of camaraderie is comforting, it's essential to remember that the true strength of a belief lies not just in group consensus but in the quality of evidence supporting it.

Empowerment to Think Critically
The key to strengthening your understanding of any conspiracy theory is the ability to think independently and critically. It's not about blindly agreeing with what everyone else believes, whether that's the mainstream narrative or the alternative views within your group. True critical thinkers question everything—including the voices within their community.

One of the dangers of group dynamics is that it can create echo chambers where only reinforcing ideas are shared. This can make it difficult to see the full picture, as dissenting opinions or contradictory evidence are often ignored or ridiculed. To avoid falling into this trap, you should actively seek out opposing viewpoints and challenge them on their merits. Rather than dismissing mainstream information outright, critically evaluate it. Are there credible points? How does this evidence stack up against your theory? By understanding both sides, you build stronger arguments.

Conspiracy theories are often complex and involve connecting seemingly unrelated events. By engaging with the theory critically, you ensure you're not just connecting dots because they fit the narrative you prefer but because they make logical sense. Take pride in refining your thoughts—this is where real empowerment comes from. When you critically assess every angle of a theory, you're not just a follower of an idea; you're someone who understands the nuances and can defend your position with clarity.

As you explore conspiracy theories, ask yourself: "What would it take for me to change my mind?" If your belief system is built on strong foundations, challenging those beliefs makes them more robust. You don't weaken your stance by questioning your assumptions and being open to other explanations—you solidify it. If your theory withstands tough scrutiny, it becomes much harder for others to tear it down.

Tools for Strengthening Arguments

The power of any argument lies in the quality of evidence and the clarity with which you can present it. To be taken seriously in any debate or discussion, your arguments must be well-supported, well-reasoned, and free from obvious logical fallacies. Below are some tools and techniques to help you build stronger, more compelling arguments:

1. Diversify Your Information Sources: It's easy to rely on several alternative news outlets, social media influencers, or online forums for information. While these sources may align with your views, they can create an echo chamber that limits your perspective. To build stronger arguments, you need to research across a broad range of sources, including those that may challenge your views. This doesn't mean accepting the mainstream narrative at face value but understanding it deeply enough to critique it effectively. If you can engage with opposing viewpoints knowledgeably, your arguments will be more persuasive.

2. Scrutinize Your Evidence: Theories are only as strong as the evidence supporting them. Take the time to fact-check claims, verify sources, and ensure that your evidence is credible. Avoid cherry-picking data—where only the facts that support your argument are highlighted, and contradicting evidence is ignored. A balanced approach shows intellectual honesty and strengthens your position. When presenting your theory, include evidence that challenges it and explain why it's insufficient to disprove your stance. This demonstrates that you've thought through all angles.

3. Use Logical Structures: Structure your arguments logically so they're easy to follow. Start with a clear thesis, back it up with well-sourced evidence, and address counterarguments directly. Logical fallacies like ad hominem attacks (criticizing the person rather than the argument) or strawman arguments (misrepresenting an opposing view to make it easier to attack) weaken your case. Avoid them at all costs. Instead, focus on crafting an argument that is both internally consistent and supported by verifiable facts.

4. Think Long-Term: Sometimes, conspiracy theories are hard to prove conclusively in the short term. However, you can use this to your advantage instead of being discouraged. Position your argument within a broader context that allows for long-term investigation. For instance, if there's limited evidence now, focus on patterns of behavior or long-term trends that support your theory. This makes your argument less reliant on a single piece of evidence and harder to dismiss outright.

5. Stay Calm, Stay Focused: Avoid emotional appeals or inflammatory rhetoric. Conspiracy theories often elicit strong emotions, but to gain credibility, you must present your case calmly and rationally. Keep your tone focused on facts and evidence rather than attacking opposing views emotionally. A level-headed approach signals confidence and maturity, which strengthens your overall position.

6. Use Questions to Your Advantage: Ask provocative, thoughtful questions instead of always making bold claims. Questions can sometimes be more powerful than statements, as they challenge others to think critically and draw conclusions. For example, rather than stating, "Elites orchestrated this global event," you could ask, "Why do we see the same powerful figures benefiting from these crises repeatedly?" This technique engages the audience and invites them to explore the answers themselves.

By empowering yourself to think critically and using these tools to strengthen your arguments, you position yourself as a thoughtful and credible voice in the world of conspiracy theories. Instead of being swayed by the loudest voices or the most dramatic claims, you can contribute reasoned, well-supported insights that challenge others to think more deeply. The aim is not to abandon your beliefs but to refine them so they stand on the firmest possible ground.

In a world filled with misinformation and hidden agendas, the ability to think critically and construct solid, evidence-based arguments is your best defense—and your greatest strength. When you embrace these practices, you transform from a passive consumer of conspiracy theories into an active, empowered participant in the quest for truth.

Balancing Individuality and Group Identity

One of the challenges many conspiracy theorists face is balancing the powerful sense of belonging within a like-minded community with the need to maintain intellectual independence. It's easy to get caught up in the echo chamber, where the same ideas circulate without much scrutiny or challenge. However, as a critical thinker who values investigative research, maintaining individuality while participating in these groups is essential for developing unique insights and contributing fresh perspectives. This balance can enhance your role within the community and make your voice stand out as someone offering more than just recycled theories.

The first step to achieving this balance is recognizing the group's dynamics and identifying where your thoughts and interpretations diverge from the mainstream. Ask yourself: Am I simply repeating what others are saying, or am I adding something new to the conversation? It's easy to default to collective thinking when you're surrounded by people who agree with you, but this can limit your personal growth and understanding. By consciously reflecting on where your beliefs may differ, you open up space for creativity and critical thinking, allowing you to contribute a perspective others might overlook.

Challenging ideas within the community can feel risky, especially if it contradicts the group's consensus. However, through questioning—even within friendly circles—you strengthen your arguments and introduce novel approaches. Instead of being a passive participant, push yourself to discuss new questions or counterpoints that others may not have considered. For instance, when someone presents a widely accepted theory, consider playing devil's advocate—not to disprove it, but to test its strength. By doing this, you demonstrate that you are a deep thinker capable of considering multiple angles, and your peers will respect the fact that you're bringing new depth to discussions.

Another effective way to maintain individuality is by seeking out new sources of information outside your immediate community's typical content. While it's natural to be drawn to sources that align with your beliefs, limiting yourself to these can stunt your intellectual growth. Broadening your research and looking into alternative explanations or lesser-known theories can give you unique insights you can bring back to the group.

This makes you a resource for fresh information, enhancing your community value while remaining aligned with your core beliefs.

It's also helpful to cultivate a sense of intellectual curiosity. People who stand out in any community are those who ask the right questions, not necessarily those who have all the answers. Embrace the unknown by admitting where gaps exist in your understanding and being open to learning from diverse sources, even those that initially seem to contradict your current views. This openness reinforces your intellectual independence and positions you as someone constantly evolving—a key trait in maintaining respect and influence within any community.

Lastly, it's important to remember that true leadership often emerges from those willing to question the status quo, even within their ranks. If you can confidently introduce new theories or interpretations—backed by thoughtful research and critical analysis—you can help shape the community's direction rather than simply following it. People are naturally drawn to original thinkers, and by cultivating this role, you strengthen your identity within the group, making your contributions valuable and influential.

Balancing individuality with group identity is an ongoing process, but it strengthens both your personal beliefs and your community's overall discussions. By standing firm in your independent thought, while participating in collective conversation, you enrich the group's understanding and establish yourself as a respected, critical voice. In doing so, you ensure that you're not just echoing the voices of others but helping to drive the conversation forward in meaningful, impactful ways.

Exploring Emotions in Conspiracy Beliefs

When discussing conspiracy theories, we often focus on the evidence, logic, and reasoning behind the ideas, but there's another powerful force driving belief: emotions. The emotional component of conspiracy beliefs is just as important—if not more so—than the intellectual side. Fear, anger, frustration, and hope can deeply influence people's engagement with these theories. Understanding the role emotions play helps you see why conspiracy theories are so compelling. It gives you the tools to manage those feelings and use them to fuel your intellectual curiosity rather than cloud your judgment.

Emotions as Strengths in Conspiracy Beliefs

At their core, emotions can drive curiosity and motivate you to seek out the truth. The emotional spark you feel when first encountering a theory—whether it's indignation at a perceived injustice, fear of a hidden threat, or even excitement at uncovering something others don't see—often plays a critical role in pushing you to explore further. It's not wrong to feel deeply about these issues. In fact, it's often this emotional investment that fuels some of the most passionate and thorough research.

For instance, anger at governmental corruption or media manipulation may make you question mainstream narratives and search for alternative sources of information. Fear of losing control over your life can lead to questioning authority, making you more critical of policies or hidden agendas. These emotional responses push you to look beyond the surface and find answers that satisfy your need for understanding.

Emotions like hope or optimism can also be a powerful motivator. Hope for a better world or exposing the truth can inspire you to dig deeper into theories that seem to offer solutions. When a conspiracy theory aligns with a desire to see justice or freedom, the emotional drive behind that theory can create a sense of purpose and even community as you find others who share your feelings.

Recognizing these emotions as part of the process can empower you. By acknowledging that your feelings are driving your curiosity, you can harness them as a strength. They don't have to cloud your judgment; they can sharpen your focus. After all, your emotional investment in a theory often keeps you pushing forward even when the evidence seems complicated, or the answers aren't immediately clear.

The Vulnerability of Emotion

That said, emotions can also be a double-edged sword. When you're deeply emotionally invested in a belief, it becomes harder to accept contradictory information. This is because emotions often override logic. If you've felt anger or fear toward a certain group or institution, your brain might instinctively reject anything that suggests you're not guilty of wrongdoing. When this happens, it becomes difficult to engage in critical thinking because your emotional reactions shut down your openness to alternative explanations.

For example, fear can lead to paranoia. If you're constantly anxious about hidden threats or dangers, it's easy to see every piece of information as part of a bigger plot. This can make you more susceptible to connecting random dots or believing in increasingly complex conspiracies that confirm your fears. Similarly, if you're angry at a particular figure or institution, your emotions might cause you to overlook reasonable counterarguments because you want to validate your anger.

Emotional vulnerability is especially dangerous in echo chambers, where the same ideas and feelings are constantly reinforced. In these spaces, emotions can become exaggerated. Instead of using your feelings as a tool for curiosity, others can manipulate them to keep you in a heightened state of fear, anger, or distrust. This makes it even harder to critically evaluate the evidence because your emotional attachment to the theory grows stronger the longer you remain in that environment.

Managing Emotions to Strengthen Beliefs
So, how do you manage these emotions without letting them control you? It starts with self-awareness. Recognize when you feel particularly emotional about a theory and ask yourself why. Are you feeling angry because of an experience that clouds your judgment? Are you afraid of something that's out of your control? By identifying the root of your emotions, you can separate them from the facts at hand.

Once you know your emotional triggers, you can use them to your advantage. Instead of letting fear or anger dictate your beliefs, allow those emotions to motivate you to find better, more comprehensive evidence. Channel your emotional investment into thorough research. Ask yourself, "If I'm feeling this strongly about a theory, what would I need to see to feel more confident in my belief?" By focusing on the quality of the evidence rather than the intensity of your emotions, you ensure that your arguments remain logical and grounded, even if your feelings are strong.

Another useful strategy is to step back and evaluate the role emotions play in the community around you. Are other people in your conspiracy theory group feeding off each other's fear or anger? Are these emotions clouding their ability to think critically? Sometimes, taking a moment to step outside the group dynamic and reflect on your feelings can help you regain perspective. If you see that emotions are escalating, make an effort to focus on evidence-based discussions rather than purely emotional ones.

Emotional Resilience in the Face of Doubt
Managing your emotions doesn't mean suppressing them. It means building emotional resilience—facing doubt or contradictory information without feeling personally attacked or destabilized. This resilience is crucial when your beliefs are challenged. Emotional resilience allows you to engage calmly and rationally instead of reacting defensively or emotionally when someone questions your theory.

This strengthens your position in debates and reinforces your intellectual independence. You're no longer simply reacting to the world but actively analyzing it. When your emotions are in check, you're less likely to be swayed by fear-mongering or sensational claims that prey on vulnerability. Instead, you can calmly assess the facts and adjust your beliefs as necessary.

Embracing Emotional Curiosity
Finally, emotions can be a powerful driver of intellectual curiosity. Rather than trying to suppress feelings like fear or excitement, embrace them as part of the journey. Use them to ask deeper questions and explore more complex theories. If you're afraid of something, ask why that fear exists and where it originated. If you're hopeful about a particular outcome, dig deeper into what it would take to achieve that reality.

By controlling your emotions and using them as tools for discovery, you can maintain a balanced approach to conspiracy theories. Emotional investment doesn't have to lead to naive belief—it can fuel critical thinking and empower you to explore deeper truths.

Analyzing Emotional Triggers

- **Reflect on Your Emotional Triggers:** What emotions drive your interest in specific conspiracy theories? Is it fear, anger, hope, or something else? How do these emotions shape your beliefs?

- **Managing Emotions in Discussions:** Think about how you handle emotional reactions when discussing your theories with others. Are there moments when your emotions cloud your ability to see the evidence clearly?

- **Channeling Emotions Productively:** How can you use your emotional investment in conspiracy theories to fuel intellectual curiosity rather than unquestioning belief?

Understanding the role of emotions in your beliefs helps you manage your reactions and makes you a more resilient and empowered thinker. By balancing your emotional triggers with critical thinking, you can build stronger, more credible arguments that stand up to scrutiny—both from others and yourself.

CHAPTER 13

INTERCONNECTED THEORIES AND PATTERNS

IMAGINE SURFING THE WEB late at night and stumbling upon a forum discussing various conspiracy theories. As you read through the posts, you begin to notice a pattern. Despite the different topics—ranging from government cover-ups to secret societies—the theories often share common elements. This chapter explores those recurring themes and how they weave complex, interconnected narratives.

Many conspiracy theories revolve around secretive groups or shadowy elites pulling the strings behind the scenes. The Illuminati, often cited as a secret society with a hidden agenda, is a prime example. Believed to have been disbanded in the 18th century, the Illuminati is frequently resurrected in modern theories as a clandestine organization manipulating global events. Similarly, the concept of the Deep State suggests a group of unelected bureaucrats and officials who wield power behind the scenes, influencing government policies and decisions without public knowledge. We discussed several other secret societies in Chapter 11, all with similar goals. These theories share a common thread: the belief that powerful, unseen forces are shaping the world, often to the detriment of the general public.

Hidden agendas and covert operations are another recurring theme in conspiracy theories. The CIA's MKUltra project, which aimed to explore mind control through various means is often cited as evidence of the government's willingness to engage in secretive and ethically dubious activities. HAARP, the High-Frequency Active Auroral Research Program, is another example. While officially described as a research program, it has been accused of being a tool for weather manipulation and even mind control. These theories suggest that governments and secret organizations are hiding their true intentions and actively engaging in covert operations that could have far-reaching consequences.

Manipulation of public perception and media control is another common motif. The idea that the media is controlled by powerful interests to shape public opinion is a cornerstone of many conspiracy theories. Whether it's the notion that mainstream news outlets are suppressing important stories or that entertainment media is embedding subliminal messages, the underlying belief is that what we see and hear is carefully curated to serve hidden agendas. This belief is often coupled with the idea that independent media and whistleblowers are the only "real" information sources, further entrenching distrust in mainstream narratives.

Overarching narratives often serve to connect these disparate elements into a cohesive whole. One of the most pervasive is the concept of the New World Order (NWO), which posits that a global elite is working to establish a totalitarian world government. This theory ties together various conspiracies, suggesting that everything from financial crises to wars and pandemics is orchestrated to bring about this new order. The Federal Reserve, UN Agenda 21, and the Bilderberg Group are frequently implicated as tools or meetings of this shadowy elite. For example, proponents of the NWO theory argue that the Federal Reserve manipulates the economy to create crises that justify increased government control, while Agenda 21 is viewed as a blueprint for global governance under the guise of sustainable development.

The cultural and historical context also plays a significant role in shaping and interrelating conspiracy theories. The paranoia of the Cold War era, with its spies and secret operations, laid fertile ground for theories about government cover-ups and espionage. The Red Scare and McCarthyism further fueled suspicions of hidden communist agendas within the U.S. government, leaving a lasting impact on American society's collective psyche.

Technological advancements, particularly the rise of the internet and social media, have transformed the landscape of conspiracy theories. The internet provides a platform for rapid information dissemination, allowing theories to spread quickly and gain traction. Social media algorithms that maximize engagement often prioritize sensational content, creating echo chambers where conspiracy theories can thrive.

For example, the heightened security measures implemented post-9/11 have fueled interconnected theories about terrorism, government surveillance, and civil liberties. The Patriot Act, with its expanded surveillance powers, is often cited as evidence of a government intent on monitoring its citizens under the pretext of national security. This ties into broader theories about a surveillance state, where every move is tracked, and personal freedoms are eroded in the name of safety. Enter Bitcoin, another tool thought to have been created as a tracking device.

Influential figures and organizations are critical in promoting and linking various conspiracies. Conspiracy theorists and thought leaders like Alex Jones have built platforms that connect multiple theories into a unified narrative. Jones's Infowars, for example, links theories about government cover-ups, secret societies, and global elites into a cohesive story that appeals to a broad audience. Alternative media outlets and social media platforms amplify these messages, reaching millions and reinforcing the interconnected nature of these theories. The role of these influencers cannot be overstated, as they often act as gatekeepers and amplifiers, shaping how theories are presented and received by the public.

In conclusion, the interconnected nature of conspiracy theories creates a complex web of narratives that share common elements, are shaped by historical and cultural contexts, and are amplified by influential figures and modern technology. Understanding these connections is crucial for navigating the often murky waters of conspiracy theories and developing a more critical and informed perspective.

Patterns in Government Cover-Ups

When you think of government cover-ups, certain patterns often emerge. These patterns involve strategies aimed at discrediting whistleblowers and dissenters, manipulating or withholding information from the public, and employing misinformation to obscure the truth. One of the most common tactics is to discredit those who come forward with incriminating information. Whistleblowers often face intense scrutiny and are labeled as unreliable or even traitorous. This tactic serves not only to undermine their credibility but also to deter others from speaking out. For example, during the Watergate scandal, attempts were made to discredit Deep Throat, the anonymous informant who provided crucial information to journalists Bob Woodward and Carl Bernstein. By casting doubt on the whistleblower's motives and reliability, the government aimed to divert attention from the scandal itself.

Another frequent strategy is manipulating or withholding information. Governments often control the flow of information to shape public perception. By selectively releasing data or crafting narratives, they can steer the public away from inconvenient truths. Misinformation is a powerful tool in this arsenal, allowing governments to muddy the waters and create confusion. During the Watergate scandal, misinformation was rampant. The Nixon administration employed various tactics to mislead the public, including the dissemination of false narratives designed to downplay the seriousness of the break-in and subsequent cover-up. These efforts aimed to create doubt and uncertainty, making it harder for the public to discern the truth.

Psychological and sociological factors also play a significant role in the persistence of cover-up theories. Distrust in authority, often borne out of past scandals and deceptions, fuels the belief that governments are always hiding something. Cognitive biases, such as confirmation bias, reinforce this belief. When people already suspect foul play, they are more likely to interpret ambiguous evidence as proof of a conspiracy. For instance, the assassination of JFK has long been a fertile ground for conspiracy theories. Despite *investigations* affirming that Lee Harvey Oswald acted alone, many people remain convinced of a broader plot. Confirmation bias plays a key role here, as individuals distrusting the government are more likely to accept alternative explanations that align with their preexisting beliefs.

Examining case studies of alleged and confirmed government cover-ups provides further insight into these patterns. The Tuskegee Syphilis Study is a notorious example of a confirmed cover-up. For decades, the U.S. Public Health Service conducted an unethical study on African American men with syphilis, withholding treatment to observe the disease's progression. This case exemplifies the manipulation of information and the lengths to which a government might go to hide unethical practices. Similarly, MKUltra, the CIA's mind control program, involved secret experiments on unwitting subjects, further illustrating the theme of covert operations and hidden agendas.

On the other hand, alleged cover-ups like 9/11 insider knowledge and the Roswell incident continue to captivate the public imagination. The theory that elements within the U.S. government had prior knowledge of the 9/11 attacks but chose not to act is rooted in the same distrust that fuels other conspiracy theories. The Roswell incident, involving claims of a crashed UFO and subsequent government cover-up, taps into fears of hidden technological advancements and extraterrestrial encounters. Both cases fit into broader patterns of government secrecy and the manipulation of public perception.

The impact of government cover-ups on public trust and policy is profound. Each revelation of a cover-up erodes trust in governmental institutions, making people more skeptical of official narratives. This erosion of trust can lead to political and social movements advocating for greater transparency and accountability. The rise of whistleblower protections and freedom of information laws directly respond to public demand for more open governance. For instance, the Freedom of Information Act (FOIA) in the United States was enacted in part due to the public's desire for greater access to government records, spurred by scandals like Watergate and the Pentagon Papers. These laws aim to check government power, allowing citizens to request and receive information that might otherwise remain hidden.

The influence of cover-up theories extends beyond policy changes. They shape public discourse and contribute to a climate of suspicion and skepticism. While this can be healthy in moderation, fostering critical thinking and vigilance, it can also lead to cynicism and disengagement. When people feel that they cannot trust their government, they may become less likely to participate in civic activities, such as voting or community organizing. This disengagement can weaken democratic institutions and make it easier for those in power to operate without accountability.

Understanding these patterns in government cover-ups sheds light on more than just concealed agendas; it reveals a strategy that seems designed not only to achieve the immediate goals of those in power but also to sow seeds of distrust and disengagement among the public. By blurring the line between fact and fiction and fueling skepticism, these actions lead many to question and withdraw from the democratic process—an outcome that may very well serve the interests of those who benefit from a distracted and disillusioned population. It's a cycle that deepens with each revelation, suggesting that cultivating distrust could be part of the agenda itself.

From Watchdogs to Gatekeepers

In the past, the media was celebrated as the public's watchdog, a relentless investigator committed to uncovering hidden truths and exposing corruption. Journalists were seen as truth-seekers, champions of the people whose work held powerful institutions accountable. The Pentagon Papers provide a clear example of this role—when The New York Times published classified documents revealing that the U.S. government had misled the public about the Vietnam War, it reinforced the media's role in democratic society as an essential check on government.

However, the relationship between the media and those in power has shifted dramatically over the years. Today, many believe that media organizations are less committed to uncovering hidden truths and more aligned with the interests of the elite. Instead of challenging powerful figures or exposing corruption, modern media outlets often appear to serve as amplifiers for official narratives, carefully curating information to support established agendas. This evolution has turned what was once an essential part of democracy into an instrument that many see as part of the problem.

At the heart of this transformation is the concentration of media ownership. Just a few corporations now control a significant portion of news outlets worldwide, creating an environment where diverse perspectives are increasingly rare. The result is a media landscape that often prioritizes sensationalism over substance, pushing stories that serve the interests of their corporate owners or sponsors. In this environment, coverage of complex issues is reduced to simplified soundbites, and topics that threaten the status quo are often ignored or dismissed as "fringe."

This shift has led to a growing perception that the media is complicit in obscuring the truth rather than revealing it. Take, for instance, the lead-up to the Iraq War, where major outlets uncritically echoed government claims about weapons of mass destruction, setting the stage for a conflict based on faulty information. Or consider the media's handling of controversial surveillance programs, which were downplayed or framed as necessary measures for public safety, rather than as violations of privacy rights. In cases like these, the media has helped to perpetuate official narratives while neglecting its duty to question and scrutinize.

The rise of digital media and social media platforms has disrupted the media landscape, offering a space where alternative voices and independent journalists can challenge official narratives. However, rather than embracing these platforms as avenues for genuine discourse, mainstream media often attempts to discredit or censor these voices, framing them as sources of misinformation. This response underscores the lengths to which the establishment will go to maintain control over the dominant narrative, pushing back against any challenge to their carefully curated version of events.

In this landscape, it's not surprising that alternative media and independent investigative journalists have gained followings by positioning themselves as the "real" truth-tellers, unbound by corporate interests. For many, these sources represent a return to the media's original mission—to seek truth without fear or favor. Yet, even as these voices gain traction, they are often met with swift discrediting by mainstream outlets, further fueling the perception that the media is intent on silencing any narrative that diverges from the official line.

The transformation of the media from a check on power to, arguably, a participant in cover-ups is one of the most troubling shifts of our time. Once heralded as a beacon of truth, today's media has become just another layer of obfuscation. The public is left to sift through layers of bias and omission, seeking the truth on their own, often turning to sources outside the traditional media landscape.

In a world where the media no longer serves as the investigative force it once was, the burden of questioning, of searching, and of unearthing hidden truths falls increasingly on the individual. This shift has left many to wonder whether the media's role is still to inform—or if it has become just another tool in the hands of those who would rather certain truths remain hidden.

The convergence of these patterns—government cover-ups, covert power structures, and a media that appears more interested in preserving narratives than challenging them—paints a concerning picture of modern society. Once the institutions that were supposed to question authority and provide transparency are themselves absorbed into a cycle of control, the true power lies not in the government alone but in a web of influence that keeps certain truths just out of reach.

For those who are willing to look past the surface and explore what lies beneath, the responsibility of piecing together these threads has never been more important. In this era, the search for truth is no longer about passive trust but about active pursuit. It's a journey that requires discerning what is real from what is fed, challenging the voices that claim authority, and fostering a critical lens that remains resilient even when the answers are elusive. In a world increasingly shadowed by unseen forces, the call to question and investigate isn't just an option—it may well be the most essential path forward.

Keeping the Curiosity Alive

As we approach the final chapters, I hope this guide has sparked your curiosity and provided valuable insights into the world of conspiracy theories. Your feedback can make a big difference! By leaving an honest review on Amazon, you'll help other truth-seekers discover this book and dive deeper into these mysteries.

Thank you for contributing to our community of inquisitive minds. Your support ensures more people can explore and benefit from the eye-opening revelations and intriguing theories we've discussed.

Simply click or scan the QR code below to leave your review on Amazon. It only takes a minute, but your impact could help uncover more truths.

CHAPTER 14

WHEN THEORY BECOMES REALITY

REAL CONSPIRACIES HAVE FUELED the enduring belief in hidden agendas and secret plots throughout history. While many conspiracy theories may seem far-fetched or speculative, some have their roots in events where governments, institutions, and powerful figures engaged in deception, cover-ups, and unethical actions. These verified conspiracies reveal that not all theories are born from paranoia; some arise from the historical reality that those in power can and do conspire. In this chapter, we'll touch on several notable instances where conspiracy theories turned out to be true, illustrating how the shadow of secrecy in the past continues to influence how we view the world today.

Early Foundations (Pre-Cold War)

The Dreyfus Affair (1894-1906)
The Dreyfus Affair, a political scandal in late 19th-century France, involved the wrongful conviction of Jewish army officer Alfred Dreyfus for treason. Dreyfus was accused of passing military secrets to the Germans, but evidence later revealed that the true culprit was another officer. Dreyfus's wrongful conviction was fueled by anti-Semitic sentiment within the French military and government.

The affair divided French society, with Dreyfus supporters (the Dreyfusards) advocating for his exoneration, while his opponents (the anti-Dreyfusards) clung to the false narrative of his guilt. Ultimately, Dreyfus was pardoned, but the case exposed deep-seated prejudices and corruption in the French establishment.

Big Tobacco's Cover-up (1950s-1990s)
Big Tobacco's cover-up is one of modern history's most infamous examples of corporate deception. For decades, tobacco companies were aware of the harmful effects of smoking but deliberately concealed this information from the public. Internal documents revealed

that as early as the 1950s, executives knew that nicotine was addictive and that smoking caused serious health issues, including cancer and heart disease. Despite this knowledge, they launched aggressive marketing campaigns to downplay the risks, often using misleading information and false science to claim that smoking was safe or, at the very least, not conclusively harmful.

In the 1990s, a wave of lawsuits and investigative journalism finally exposed the full extent of the tobacco industry's cover-up. Whistleblowers from within the industry came forward, providing evidence that Big Tobacco had manipulated scientific research, marketed cigarettes to children, and systematically denied the dangers of smoking. This led to landmark legal settlements, including the 1998 Master Settlement Agreement, in which the tobacco companies agreed to pay billions of dollars in healthcare costs and fund anti-smoking campaigns. The revelations about Big Tobacco's deceit had a lasting impact on public health policy and corporate accountability, showing the lengths companies will go to protect profits over people's well-being.

The tobacco industry's deception went beyond simply hiding evidence. They actively worked to create uncertainty about the health risks of smoking, pioneering tactics that would later be adopted by other industries facing similar scrutiny. The concept of "manufacturing doubt" became a template for corporations dealing with inconvenient scientific findings. The pharmaceutical industry, for instance, has employed many of the same strategies first perfected by Big Tobacco: funding questionable research, attacking the credibility of independent scientists, and emphasizing uncertainty in public debates. The tobacco conspiracy thus not only affected public health but also provided a playbook for future corporate deception.

Cold War Era Beginnings

As the world emerged from World War II, the dawn of the Cold War ushered in an era of unprecedented secrecy and paranoia. The threat of nuclear annihilation and the ideological battle between capitalism and communism created an environment where governments justified increasingly extreme measures in the name of national security. This period saw some of the most egregious examples of government overreach as the line between protecting and controlling citizens became dangerously blurred.

Operation Mockingbird (1950s-1970s)

Operation Mockingbird was a CIA program during the Cold War aimed at manipulating media narratives. Evidence suggests that the agency recruited journalists to spread propaganda and influence public opinion in favor of U.S. interests. Though details remain classified, there is significant documentation showing the CIA's engagement in efforts to control media both domestically and internationally.

Declassified documents show that the CIA had close relationships with major news outlets and journalists, raising questions about the true extent of the agency's influence on the press. Although Operation Mockingbird remains partly shrouded in mystery, its existence underscores concerns about media manipulation and government influence over the flow of information.

Project Sunshine (1953-1970s)
Project Sunshine was a secret research initiative conducted by the U.S. government in the 1950s to study the effects of nuclear radiation on humans, particularly after atomic bomb tests. The project aimed to understand the impact of radioactive fallout on human tissue, especially in infants and young children, who were believed to be more vulnerable to radiation exposure. However, the true scope of the project was kept hidden from the public, and it was later revealed that scientists and government officials had been collecting tissue samples, including bones from deceased children, without the consent of their families.

The unethical nature of Project Sunshine sparked outrage once it came to light in the 1990s. Families were horrified to learn that their loved ones' remains had been used in government experiments without their knowledge. The project exposed the dark side of Cold War-era scientific research, where pursuing knowledge about nuclear fallout was prioritized over human rights and ethical considerations. The scandal forced the government to confront its history of secret and unethical experiments, raising awareness about the need for stricter ethical standards in scientific research.

MKUltra (1953-1973)
MKUltra was a secret CIA program that ran from the 1950s to the early 1970s, aimed at developing mind control techniques. The program involved experiments on unwitting U.S. and Canadian citizens, using drugs like LSD, sensory deprivation, and electroshock therapy in an attempt to manipulate and control human behavior. MKUltra's goal was to find methods for interrogations, psychological warfare, and brainwashing during the Cold War.

The extent of MKUltra's abuses was uncovered in the 1970s when investigations by the Church Committee and the Rockefeller Commission revealed the horrifying details.

Although many documents were destroyed in 1973, the surviving evidence showed that the CIA had violated human rights on a vast scale, conducting unethical and dangerous experiments that left many participants with long-lasting trauma. MKUltra remains one of the most infamous examples of a government conspiracy with chilling implications for the misuse of power.

The revelation of MKUltra's existence had far-reaching implications beyond the immediate scandal. It fundamentally changed how Americans viewed their government and sparked a cultural shift that still reverberates. The program has inspired countless books, movies, and T.V. shows, embedding itself in popular culture as a shorthand for government manipulation and unethical experimentation. More significantly, it raised crucial questions about the limits of state power: If the government could secretly drug its citizens, what else might it be capable of? The legacy of MKUltra serves as a chilling reminder that even in democratic societies, unchecked power can lead to profound abuses.

Medical Experimentation and Race

The Cold War era's ethical transgressions weren't limited to mind control and surveillance. Some of the most disturbing conspiracies involved medical experimentation, particularly on vulnerable and marginalized populations. These experiments, often conducted under the guise of public health initiatives, reveal a darker aspect of medical history—one where scientific advancement was prioritized over human dignity and consent. The racial dimensions of these studies also expose how existing societal prejudices influenced which groups were deemed expendable in the pursuit of medical knowledge.

The Tuskegee Syphilis Study (1932-1972)

The Tuskegee Syphilis Study is one of the most notorious examples of government conspiracy. Conducted between 1932 and 1972, this study involved the U.S. Public Health Service observing the natural progression of untreated syphilis in African American men. The participants, mostly poor and uneducated, were told they were receiving free healthcare when, in reality, they were being deceived. Treatment was deliberately withheld, even after penicillin was proven effective in curing syphilis in the 1940s.

The experiment continued for decades, leading to unnecessary suffering and death among the men and their families. The truth came to light in 1972 after a whistleblower exposed the study, sparking public outrage. This scandal significantly damaged trust in public health institutions, particularly in African American communities. It led to reforms in medical ethics and the establishment of institutional review boards to ensure the ethical treatment of human subjects in research.

Guatemala STD Experiments (1946-1948)

The Guatemala STD Experiments, conducted by the U.S. government in the late 1940s, stand as one of the darkest chapters in medical experimentation. Between 1946 and 1948, researchers working with the U.S. Public Health Service intentionally infected thousands of Guatemalans with sexually transmitted diseases, including syphilis and gonorrhea. The subjects, many of whom were prisoners, mental health patients, and soldiers, were not informed about the true nature of the experiments. Doctors deliberately exposed them to the diseases, often through direct injection or by arranging for infected individuals to engage in sexual contact with uninfected subjects. The stated goal of the experiments was to study how sexually transmitted infections spread and to test the efficacy of penicillin as a treatment.

This horrific experimentation remained hidden for decades until it was uncovered by a researcher in 2010. The revelation sparked international outrage and led to formal apologies from the U.S. and Guatemalan governments. In 2010, President Barack Obama personally called the Guatemalan president to express regret, and then-Secretary of State Hillary Clinton also issued an apology. Unlike other medical scandals, such as the Tuskegee Syphilis Study, which involved withholding treatment, the Guatemala experiments involved the deliberate infection of vulnerable populations, making it an even more egregious violation of human rights. The exposure of these experiments has raised important ethical questions about medical research and reinforced the need for strict oversight to prevent such abuses from happening again.

Domestic Surveillance and Control

COINTELPRO (1956-1971)

COINTELPRO, short for Counter Intelligence Program, was an FBI initiative from 1956 to 1971 aimed at surveilling, infiltrating, discrediting, and disrupting domestic political organizations deemed subversive. Targets included civil rights groups like the Black Panther Party, feminist movements, anti-Vietnam War protestors, and even Dr. Martin Luther King Jr. The FBI engaged in illegal tactics such as wiretapping, spreading false information, and sowing internal divisions within these groups.

The program was kept secret until the early 1970s when activists broke into an FBI office in Media, Pennsylvania, and uncovered documents exposing COINTELPRO. Public outrage followed, and the program was officially disbanded, although its revelations had a lasting impact on the American public's trust in government institutions. The exposure of COINTELPRO highlighted the extent to which the government would go to suppress political dissent.

The Church Committee Hearings (1975)

The Church Committee hearings, held in the mid-1970s, exposed widespread abuses by U.S. intelligence agencies, including the FBI, CIA, and NSA. The hearings revealed a host of illegal activities, from assassination attempts on foreign leaders to spying on U.S. citizens. Notably, the CIA's involvement in coup attempts and the FBI's COINTELPRO operations were brought to light.

The committee's findings led to significant reforms in intelligence agencies' operations, including creating the Foreign Intelligence Surveillance Court (FISC) and stronger oversight measures to prevent future abuses. The Church Committee hearings were a critical moment in holding the U.S. government accountable for its covert actions, and they remain a landmark in the history of congressional oversight.

Modern Era and International Operations

As we move into more recent history, you'll see that the nature of conspiracies evolved with the times. The advent of mass media, and later the internet, changed both how secrets could be kept and how they could be exposed. While the motivations behind these conspiracies remained similar—power, profit, political advantage—the methods and scope expanded dramatically. Modern conspiracies often involve a complex interplay between government agencies, corporate interests, and media manipulation, making them harder to execute and, paradoxically, to conceal completely.

The Gulf of Tonkin Incident (1964)

The Gulf of Tonkin Incident was a pivotal event that escalated U.S. involvement in the Vietnam War. In August 1964, the U.S. government claimed that North Vietnamese forces had attacked U.S. naval vessels in the Gulf of Tonkin, leading Congress to pass the Gulf of Tonkin Resolution, which authorized President Lyndon B. Johnson to use military force in Vietnam.

Later, it was revealed that the second attack, which had been the primary justification for the resolution, never occurred. This revelation caused a significant public outcry, as it became clear that the U.S. government had misrepresented events to justify further military action. The Gulf of Tonkin Incident remains a stark example of how misinformation can manipulate public opinion and drive foreign policy decisions.

The Iran-Contra Affair (1985-1987)

The Iran-Contra Affair was a political scandal that unfolded in the mid-1980s, revealing a complex and illegal operation conducted by members of the Reagan administration. The U.S. had secretly sold arms to Iran—despite an arms embargo—in hopes of securing the release of American hostages held by Hezbollah. The proceeds from these sales were then funneled to fund the Contra rebels in Nicaragua, who were fighting the Sandinista government. This action directly violated the Boland Amendment, which prohibited U.S. assistance to the Contras.

When the scheme was exposed in 1986, it led to widespread controversy and investigations. Key figures in the Reagan administration, including Lt. Col. Oliver North, were implicated, and several officials were convicted, although many had their sentences commuted or pardoned. The affair tarnished the Reagan administration's reputation and raised serious concerns about government transparency and accountability.

The CIA and Drug Trafficking (1980s)

In the 1980s, a major scandal broke involving the CIA and its alleged connections to drug trafficking in support of the Nicaraguan Contras. Journalist Gary Webb's series *Dark Alliance* exposed the link between the CIA-backed Contras and the crack cocaine epidemic in the United States. Webb uncovered that the CIA turned a blind eye as drug dealers sold vast amounts of cocaine in U.S. cities, with proceeds funneled back to fund the Contra rebels in Nicaragua. This revelation implicated the CIA in the drug trade and stirred massive controversy, especially in light of the devastating impact crack cocaine had on inner-city communities.

A key figure in this scandal was "Freeway" Rick Ross, a notorious drug kingpin in Los Angeles. Ross was supplied with cheap, high-quality cocaine by Nicaraguan traffickers who had connections to the CIA. Ross turned these supplies into millions of dollars by converting the cocaine into crack and flooding the streets of L.A. His empire grew alongside the crack epidemic, and while he wasn't aware of the CIA link at the time, his operations became a central part of how the drug trade funded covert U.S. operations in Central America. The scandal raised serious questions about government involvement in illicit activities and its catastrophic social consequences.

NSA Mass Surveillance (exposed 2013)

The NSA's mass surveillance program had long been a subject of speculation, with many people believing that the government was secretly collecting data on its citizens. This suspicion grew in the wake of the Patriot Act, passed in the aftermath of the 9/11 attacks, which expanded the government's powers to monitor communications in the name of national security. The program included the bulk collection of phone records, email exchanges, and internet browsing data, raising concerns about privacy and civil liberties. Critics argued that such extensive surveillance could be used not just to track potential terrorists but also to monitor ordinary citizens without their knowledge or consent.

In 2013, these concerns were confirmed when Edward Snowden, a former NSA contractor, leaked classified documents exposing the full extent of the NSA's activities. Snowden's revelations showed that the NSA had been conducting widespread surveillance, including the collection of phone metadata from millions of Americans, often without proper oversight or judicial warrants. His leaks ignited a global debate about privacy, security, and government transparency, leading to significant reforms in U.S. surveillance laws. Snowden's actions were hailed as heroic by privacy advocates and condemned as treasonous by government officials. Still, they undeniably exposed a major government conspiracy hidden from the public for years.

The NSA surveillance revelations marked a turning point in the digital age, forcing a global conversation about privacy in an interconnected world. Unlike previous government conspiracies, this one affected virtually everyone who used modern communication technology. It raised unsettling questions about privacy in the 21st century: In an era where we voluntarily share so much of our lives online, what right do we have to digital privacy? The scandal also highlighted the unique challenges whistleblowers face in the digital age. Snowden's revelations were unprecedented in scale thanks to the ease of copying digital files. Still, modern surveillance tools also made it harder for him to avoid detection and safely expose the truth.

Scientific Skepticism and Recent Developments

Gay Frogs Theory (1990s-present)

The Gay Frogs theory became infamous when Alex Jones, a prominent conspiracy theorist, claimed that chemicals in the water were "turning the frogs gay." While Jones' framing of the issue was ridiculed, a kernel of truth gave rise to this theory. Research by scientist

Dr. Tyrone Hayes found that atrazine, a widely used pesticide, could cause hormonal disruptions in amphibians, leading to the feminization of male frogs.

Although initially dismissed as a fringe theory, concerns about atrazine's impact have since gained traction in the scientific community. Research has begun to reveal that the chemical's effects may extend beyond amphibians to other species, potentially affecting mammals and raising legitimate concerns for human health and broader environmental safety. Far from a mere exaggeration, the Gay Frogs theory now underscores serious questions about the unchecked influence of such chemicals on ecosystems and public health.

Throughout history, the truth behind these covert operations and cover-ups remained hidden for years, only to be uncovered through persistence and courage. As we've explored, these conspiracies—from unethical medical experiments to corporate deception—were not merely theoretical. They were real, with profound impacts on the people involved and society at large. What is striking about each of these cases is not just the scale of the deception but how the truth eventually emerged.

The revelation of these secrets often came through a mix of legal requests, courageous whistleblowers, investigative journalism, and congressional investigations. Documentation typically emerged years or even decades after the events occurred, sometimes through Freedom of Information Act requests that forced governments to release classified information. Whistleblowers, risking their careers and safety, stepped forward to expose hidden agendas, while relentless investigative journalists uncovered hidden truths and brought them to public attention. In many cases, official acknowledgment or apologies only came after overwhelming evidence was presented, as in the case of the Guatemala STD experiments or the NSA's mass surveillance.

Balancing Skepticism and Truth

As our exploration has shown, the landscape of conspiracy theories is far more nuanced than many might assume. Some of these theories are rooted in genuine historical events where secrecy and manipulation were not just speculation but documented reality. These verified conspiracies are powerful reminders that questioning authority and seeking hidden truths can sometimes be justified and necessary for maintaining a healthy democracy.

Yet, this reality presents us with a paradox. When genuine conspiracies are exposed, they can inadvertently fuel belief in false ones, as each revelation of government or corporate wrongdoing makes other allegations seem more plausible. The exposure of MKUltra makes mind control conspiracies more believable; the reality of corporate cover-ups like Big Tobacco's deception lends credence to other corporate conspiracy theories. This creates a unique challenge for society: how do we maintain a healthy skepticism and necessary oversight while avoiding unfounded paranoia?

The answer lies in a balanced approach:
1. Understanding historical patterns and how real conspiracies typically operate

2. Recognizing the crucial importance of evidence and documentation

3. Supporting the institutions and individuals who make exposure of real conspiracies possible—investigative journalists, whistleblowers, and independent oversight bodies

While this chapter has introduced some of the most well-known verified conspiracies, it represents only the tip of the iceberg. The lessons from these verified conspiracies remain relevant as we grapple with questions of truth, power, and secrecy in our modern world. They remind us that vigilance is necessary but must be tempered with reason and evidence. By understanding the real conspiracies that have shaped our world, we can better distinguish between justified skepticism, unfounded fear, necessary questioning, and paranoid speculation.

Conclusion

As we reach the end of this journey through some of history's most carefully concealed truths, it's clear that what lies beneath the surface is darker and more interconnected than most people would ever suspect. We've peeled back the layers of misdirection and manipulation that the media, institutions, and elites have constructed to keep the truth buried. The elite globalist agenda, cloaked in secrecy, isn't some fringe fantasy. It's a calculated, meticulously crafted operation with a singular goal: control. Control over information, control over resources, and ultimately, control over you.

Remember how we began this journey, with D.B. Cooper vanishing into that dark November sky? His disappearance wasn't just a mystery—it was a metaphor for everything that slips through the cracks of official narratives, everything that exists in the shadows of what we're told to believe. Like that Boeing 727 disappearing into the clouds, the truth often seems just beyond our grasp. But unlike the FBI agents who eventually closed Cooper's case, we refuse to accept the convenient explanations handed to us by those in power.

The mainstream media, once the watchdog for the people, has become something else entirely—a megaphone for the very powers it was supposed to challenge. Stories are carefully filtered, narratives are molded, and inconvenient truths are cast aside, rebranding the media as a gatekeeper for the elite agenda. By selectively controlling what reaches the public, they've transformed the free press into a tool of influence, used to shape opinions and keep the masses passive and pliable. The stories they choose to highlight—and those they bury—create a reality that serves their interests. Look around: how often do you see headlines questioning the very existence of a shadow elite? Or calling out the conflicts of interest between corporate sponsors and the "news" they fund?

In this book, we've explored the individuals and events that reveal the inner workings of a hidden world. Public figures who dared to defy this clandestine order—like Donald Trump—or those who became collateral damage—such as Jeffrey Epstein, whose connections to powerful individuals still spark unresolved questions—are reminders of the high stakes involved. These stories illustrate that challenging the status quo or pushing against the established narrative comes at a cost. Those who pull the strings, the elusive "they" we've referenced throughout, do not tolerate opposition lightly. Time and again, history shows us that those in power will go to great lengths to silence dissent and protect their influence, even if it means erasing threats to their meticulously crafted system.

Follow the money, and you begin to see the connections emerge, revealing a web of influence that spans governments, corporations, media, and financial institutions. The elite's power lies not just in their wealth but in their ability to manipulate policies, economies, and, ultimately, public perception. With this leverage, they've created a system that rewards loyalty and punishes resistance. Those who play by their rules rise, while those who pose a threat find themselves sidelined, discredited, or worse. This isn't paranoia—it's a pattern, a strategy that's been in play for generations.

Yet this book isn't just about laying bare their agenda; it's about empowering you with the tools to see beyond it. Knowledge, after all, is their greatest threat. When you begin to notice the patterns, recognize the connections, and question the narratives, you become harder to control. You become the anomaly in a system that thrives on obedience. As you've likely realized by now, true freedom doesn't come from following the script; it comes from rewriting it.

The question remains: What are you going to do with this awareness? Armed with the understanding of how the elite operate, how they use media to shape reality, and how they exert control over politics and society, you're now in a position to resist in ways that most can't. You've stepped beyond the veil, and there's no going back. This knowledge will change the way you see everything—the headlines, the policies, the "official" stories. Once you start to question, you'll see that the patterns repeat, each new event falling neatly into place within the broader agenda.

In every chapter, we've explored the machinations of these elites, exposing how they manipulate both events and perceptions. From financial crises to global conflicts, every move is calculated, every outcome anticipated. The ordinary citizen is just a pawn in their game, but you now know how to look beyond the surface. Keep asking yourself: Who benefits? Who profits? Who gains power? These are the questions that slice through the fog of misinformation and reveal the agenda underneath.

It's essential to remember that the elites aren't just hiding events—they're hiding the very framework by which they operate. Secret societies, clandestine meetings, and private alliances are all means to ensure that the public remains in the dark. They obscure the system itself, making it appear complex and inaccessible, so that people give up trying to understand it. But now you know that this system isn't beyond your comprehension; it's designed to look that way. The real power of the elite lies in the illusion of their invisibility. They count on people believing that such a level of coordination is impossible, that no group could wield so much influence from the shadows. But history has shown us that this level of coordination not only exists—it's the glue that holds their empire together.

As you close this book, remember that the pursuit of truth doesn't end here. This is just the beginning. The tools you've gained are now part of your arsenal. The next time you see a headline, the next time you hear an "expert" offering explanations, question everything. Don't let them pacify you with convenient lies. The pursuit of truth is never easy, but it's the only path to genuine freedom. So, stay vigilant, stay curious, and remember—truth isn't something you're given. It's something you uncover. And now that you've started down this path, you're part of a movement that will continue to grow, one question at a time.

REFLECTING AND QUESTIONING

As we close this exploration into the hidden webs of influence and control, it's clear that many official narratives mask deeper truths. This final section invites you to take a critical look at the evidence, the alternative explanations, and the lingering questions surrounding major events we've discussed. These aren't simply exercises in recounting history; they're about challenging what we're told to believe and questioning the motives behind the stories that shape our perception of reality.

In each reflection, you'll encounter thought-provoking questions meant to pierce through surface-level explanations. From the shadowy circumstances of JFK's assassination to the opaque dealings of Big Pharma, the themes here highlight a need for vigilance. As you examine each topic, ask yourself: What evidence stands out as undeniable, and what gaps remain? How do the motivations of those controlling these narratives impact your trust in institutions? Consider, too, the role of the media as a powerful tool wielded by those who shape public opinion.

These reflections aren't just a call to rethink specific events; they're a challenge to adopt a critical mindset. With each question, you'll move beyond passively accepting stories and start actively searching for what lies beneath. So, let's revisit these key moments and see how they continue to shape our understanding of truth in a world where appearances are meticulously managed.

Reflect & Question: The JFK Assassination

When examining the evidence surrounding JFK's assassination, it's crucial to revisit the infamous Zapruder film. This amateur footage captured the tragic moment frame by frame, providing a visual record that has been analyzed endlessly. Critics and proponents of various theories scrutinize the film, debating whether it shows evidence of multiple shooters or supports the lone gunman theory. As you rewatch the Zapruder film, consider the interpretations offered by experts and skeptics alike. How do their analyses shape your understanding of the event?

Eyewitness testimonies also play a pivotal role in the narrative. With over 500 people present in Dealey Plaza, their accounts vary significantly. Some claim to have heard shots from the grassy knoll, while others insist they came from the Texas School Book Depository. When assessing these testimonies, think about the reliability of human memory, especially under stress. How might the chaos and confusion of the moment have influenced these accounts?

The Warren Commission, tasked with investigating the assassination, concluded that Lee Harvey Oswald acted alone. However, its findings have faced criticism for alleged inconsistencies and omissions. Question the credibility of the Warren Commission's report. What motivations might the Commission have had for presenting a particular narrative? How do these factors influence your trust in the official account?

Alternative explanations abound, each offering a different perspective on who might have orchestrated the assassination. Some theories point to the CIA, suggesting that Kennedy's policies threatened the agency's interests. Others implicate the Mafia, angered by the Kennedy administration's crackdown on organized crime. Cuban exiles, resentful of Kennedy's handling of the Bay of Pigs invasion, also emerge as potential culprits. Reflect on these scenarios and consider how each group might have motives and means. Could the assassination have been the result of multiple conspirators working together?

The idea of multiple shooters adds another layer of complexity. The "magic bullet" theory, which posits that a single bullet caused multiple wounds to Kennedy and Governor Connally, has been a focal point of debate. Critics argue that the trajectory and wounds suggest more than one shooter. As you evaluate this theory, consider the ballistic evidence and expert analyses. How plausible do you find the idea of multiple shooters?

The assassination profoundly impacted public trust in government. It marked a turning point, fostering a sense of cynicism and suspicion that persists. The cultural and political aftermath saw a rise in conspiracy theories as people sought answers beyond the official narrative. Reflect on how this event influenced future conspiracy theories. How did it shape the way Americans view their government and its transparency?

Reflect & Question: The Moon Landing

When you examine the photographs and video footage from the Apollo missions, you might notice some alleged anomalies that have fueled the Moon Landing Hoax theory. Critics point to the American flag seemingly fluttering despite the vacuum of space, the absence of stars in the lunar sky, and shadows that appear inconsistent, suggesting artificial lighting. Experts have debunked these claims through scientific explanations. The flag's apparent movement is due to a horizontal rod holding it up, and the astronauts' handling caused the fluttering. The lack of stars results from the camera settings, which are optimized for the bright lunar surface, rendering the stars too dim to capture. Shadows appear uneven due to the Moon's rough terrain and the reflection of sunlight off the lunar surface.

Reflecting on the broader implications of the Moon Landing Hoax theory, consider what it would mean if the landings were faked. The logistics of orchestrating such a massive cover-up involving thousands of NASA employees, contractors, and international scientists seem implausible. The motivations for faking the Moon Landing would likely center around the Cold War, aiming to demonstrate technological and ideological superiority over the Soviet Union. However, sustaining this deception for over five decades, despite numerous independent validations, adds layers of complexity to the theory.

The cultural impact of the Moon Landing Hoax theory is significant. Films and documentaries often sensationalize the idea, reinforcing public skepticism. Influential figures who promote the hoax theory, like certain celebrities and conspiracy theorists, add credibility to these claims in the eyes of their followers. This has led to a persistent undercurrent of doubt despite overwhelming evidence to the contrary.

Considering the role of expert testimony, it's crucial to weigh the opinions of scientists and engineers who have dedicated their careers to space exploration. Those who support the Moon Landing provide peer-reviewed research and detailed explanations, while skeptics often rely on misinterpretations or selective evidence. The importance of peer-reviewed research in debunking myths cannot be overstated. It ensures that findings are scrutinized and validated by the scientific community, providing a robust foundation for understanding the truth.

Reflect & Question: The Deep State

Consider the evidence for the existence of the Deep State. Leaked documents and whistleblower testimonies often serve as the backbone of these claims. While some documents reveal hidden government actions, others lack credibility. For instance, the release of the Pentagon Papers unveiled significant government deception during the Vietnam War, but not all leaks carry the same weight. Examine these sources critically. Intelligence agencies like the CIA undeniably wield substantial influence over politics. Their covert operations, from the Bay of Pigs invasion to more recent interventions, showcase their capacity to shape political landscapes. But does this equate to a shadow government pulling the strings?

Reflect on the political and social implications of believing in the Deep State. This belief can erode trust in democratic institutions, leading to increased cynicism and disengagement among voters. When people think their votes don't matter because unseen forces control the government, it undermines the very foundation of democracy. How does this skepticism affect voter behavior and political engagement? Consider how it might deter participation in elections or foster support for populist leaders who promise to dismantle the so-called Deep State.

Alternative explanations for perceived government manipulation often emphasize bureaucratic inefficiencies and institutional inertia. Government actions can sometimes seem opaque and convoluted, not due to a grand conspiracy but because of red tape, miscommunication, and conflicting interests. Special interest groups and lobbying also play significant roles. These entities push their agendas, influencing policies and decisions in ways that might appear conspiratorial but are, in reality, the result of legal, albeit questionable, practices.

Analyze the influence of media and public figures in shaping the Deep State narrative. Sensationalism in media coverage can amplify paranoia and mistrust. Headlines that hint at secret plots attract readers but often lack substantiated evidence. Influential figures, from politicians to celebrities, may promote the Deep State theory for various reasons. Some seek to galvanize their base, while others aim to discredit opponents. Question their motivations. Are they driven by genuine concern or desire to manipulate public perception for personal gain? Reflect on how these dynamics shape your understanding of the Deep State and challenge you to think critically about the information you consume.

Reflect & Question: The Epstein Case

When examining Jeffrey Epstein's death, it's essential to scrutinize the autopsy reports and expert opinions. The official ruling is suicide by hanging, but pathologist Dr. Michael Baden, hired by Epstein's brother, suggests the injuries are more consistent with "homicidal strangulation." Baden points to fractures in Epstein's hyoid bone and thyroid cartilage as evidence. As you consider these differing opinions, think about the credibility of the experts and the thoroughness of the autopsy. Witness statements and security footage also play a crucial role. Epstein was found unresponsive in his cell, which had not been checked for several hours, and there were unexplained gaps in the security footage. How do these inconsistencies influence your interpretation of the events?

Reflecting on the broader implications of Epstein's case, consider how it impacts public trust in the criminal justice system. Epstein's high-profile connections and the nature of his crimes have led to widespread speculation about a cover-up to protect powerful individuals. This has fueled discussions about the influence of wealth and privilege. How does this case shape your views on the fairness and transparency of the justice system? The Epstein case also raises questions about systemic issues such as the treatment of inmates and the adequacy of prison security measures.

Alternative explanations for Epstein's death include negligence or incompetence by prison staff. The lapse in monitoring and procedural failures could indicate systemic issues rather than a deliberate cover-up. Reflect on the role of mental health issues and suicide risk factors. Epstein faced severe legal repercussions and public disgrace, which might have contributed to suicidal tendencies. Considering these factors, how plausible do you find the theory of negligence versus conspiracy?

The motivations behind promoting conspiracy theories about Epstein's death are varied. Sensationalism and media coverage amplify these theories, attracting attention and driving engagement. Political bias and agendas also play a role, with some using the case to discredit opponents or push specific narratives. Reflect on how these motivations shape public perception and your understanding of the case. Why do you think people are drawn to these theories, and how does media influence your views?

Reflect & Question: 9/11

When you scrutinize the evidence for 9/11 conspiracy theories, it's crucial to reexamine the structural engineering reports on the collapse of the Twin Towers. The National Institute of Standards and Technology (NIST) concluded that the buildings fell due to intense fires weakening the steel structure. However, some argue that the rapid, symmetrical collapse suggests controlled demolition. As you look into these reports, consider the expertise and methodologies used. First responder accounts and eyewitness testimonies also provide valuable insights. Some witnesses reported hearing explosions, fueling theories of bombs planted inside the buildings. Question the reliability of these accounts, given the chaos and confusion of the day. How might adrenaline and fear have influenced their recollections?

Reflecting on the broader implications, consider how 9/11 conspiracy theories have shaped public opinion and policy. These theories have eroded trust in government and media, fostering a climate of skepticism. This mistrust has influenced counter-terrorism policies, leading to increased surveillance and the controversial Patriot Act. Reflect on how these policies balance national security and civil liberties. Question whether the perceived threats justify the erosion of privacy. How have these theories influenced your view of governmental transparency and accountability?

Alternative explanations for perceived anomalies in the official account often point to the chaos and confusion during the attacks. Initial reports and investigations, conducted under immense pressure, might have contained errors or inconsistencies. Reflect on how these limitations could have contributed to the proliferation of conspiracy theories. Consider other plausible reasons for the anomalies, such as structural damage and fire behavior. How do these explanations compare to the more sensational claims?

The motivations behind 9/11 conspiracy theories are multifaceted. Fear and anxiety, heightened by the unprecedented nature of the attacks, drive many to seek alternative explanations. Political and ideological biases also play a role, as some use these theories to advance specific agendas. Reflect on how these motivations shape your beliefs. How does your political stance influence your interpretation of the evidence? Understanding these dynamics can help you approach the topic with a more critical and balanced perspective.

Reflect & Question: Big Pharma

Critically evaluating the evidence for Big Pharma conspiracy theories requires a deep dive into the drug development and approval processes. Pharmaceutical companies often spend years and millions of dollars developing new drugs. This includes preclinical testing on animals, multiple phases of clinical trials on humans, and rigorous scrutiny by regulatory bodies like the FDA. Despite this, some argue that the industry hides cures to maintain profits. Consider the credibility of these claims by examining case studies and legal actions. For example, the opioid crisis revealed unethical practices in marketing addictive painkillers, leading to significant legal repercussions for the companies involved. Reflect on how such instances influence your perception of Big Pharma.

The broader implications of Big Pharma conspiracy theories extend beyond individual companies. These theories can erode public trust in the healthcare system, impacting patient behavior and treatment adherence. When people doubt the motives of pharmaceutical companies, they may avoid necessary medications, opting for unproven alternatives. This skepticism can also influence regulatory policies and oversight, pushing for stricter regulations and greater transparency. Reflect on how these theories shape your views on healthcare policy and trust in medical institutions.

Exploring alternative explanations for perceived pharmaceutical misconduct, consider the role of market dynamics and profit motives. Pharmaceutical companies operate within a competitive market where profit is a driving force. This can lead to aggressive marketing tactics and prioritizing profitable treatments over less lucrative ones. Regulatory challenges and scientific uncertainty also play a role. Developing a new drug is fraught with risks; not all research leads to successful treatments. Reflect on how these factors might explain the actions of pharmaceutical companies without resorting to conspiracy theories.

Question the motivations behind Big Pharma conspiracy theories. Personal experiences and anecdotal evidence often fuel these beliefs. If someone had a negative experience with a medication or healthcare provider, they might be more inclined to distrust the industry. Media coverage and public perception also play significant roles. Sensational stories about pharmaceutical misconduct grab headlines, reinforcing the narrative of a corrupt industry. Reflect on how these influences shape your understanding of Big Pharma. Consider how media portrayal impacts your perception and whether it aligns with the broader evidence.

Reflect & Question: The Federal Reserve

When you scrutinize the evidence for Federal Reserve conspiracy theories, reexamine its ownership structure and transparency. The Federal Reserve is a complex entity with a unique blend of public and private elements. Its Board of Governors is a federal agency, while the twelve regional Reserve Banks operate as private entities. This hybrid structure has led to suspicions about who truly controls monetary policy. Critics argue that the Fed serves the interests of private bankers over the public good. Yet, the Fed publishes detailed reports, undergoes audits, and holds press conferences, aiming to maintain transparency. Consider how these factors influence your perception of its operations.

Historical reviews of the Federal Reserve's actions during economic crises provide another layer of insight. During the Great Depression, the Fed's policies were criticized for being too restrictive, exacerbating the economic downturn. In contrast, during the 2008 financial crisis, the Fed took aggressive actions, such as lowering interest rates and purchasing financial assets, to stabilize the economy. These actions were controversial but aimed at preventing a total collapse. Reflect on how these historical actions impact your trust in the Fed's ability to manage economic crises. How do these actions align with or contradict the conspiracy theories?

Theories about the Federal Reserve often influence public trust and financial policy. When people believe the Fed manipulates the economy for nefarious purposes, it erodes confidence in financial institutions. This skepticism can fuel political movements advocating for financial reform, such as the push to audit the Fed or return to the gold standard. Reflect on how these theories shape your views on financial stability and the need for oversight. Consider how the perception of economic manipulation might drive support for radical policy changes.

Alternative explanations for the Fed's actions often lie in economic theory and policy decisions. Central banks use similar tools to manage inflation, employment, and economic growth worldwide. Global economic trends and crises influence the Fed's policies, requiring nuanced and adaptive responses. Reflect on how these broader economic factors might explain the Fed's actions without resorting to conspiracy theories. Consider how economic theory and policy decisions guide their strategies, often aiming for long-term stability over short-term gains.

Reflect & Question: Secret Societies

When evaluating the evidence for secret society conspiracy theories, it is essential to examine historical documents and records. Many of these societies, like the Freemasons or the Illuminati, have extensive archives detailing their origins, rituals, and activities. Examine these documents critically. Consider the credibility of statements from historians and experts who have studied these groups. How do their findings align with the sensational claims about these societies?

Reflecting on the broader implications, think about how these theories influence public perception and behavior. The notion that secret societies control world events can significantly impact trust in political and social institutions. If people believe that a hidden group is pulling the strings, it can lead to widespread cynicism and disengagement from civic duties. This distrust can fuel anti-establishment movements, where individuals rally against perceived elitism and corruption. Reflect on how these movements gain momentum and what underlying societal issues they address.

Alternative explanations for the perceived influence of secret societies often lie in historical context and social dynamics. Many of these groups formed during significant social and political upheaval, providing a sense of community and stability. Over time, their roles and influences have evolved, often becoming more symbolic than operational. Cultural narratives and myths, perpetuated through literature and media, also play a crucial role. These stories capture the imagination and offer simple explanations for complex world events. Reflect on how these narratives shape your understanding of secret societies and their supposed control.

Question the motivations behind promoting secret society conspiracy theories. Fear and suspicion of elites often drive these beliefs. In times of economic or social instability, people seek explanations that fit their worldview. Media portrayals and popular culture further amplify these fears. Films, books, and TV shows often depict secret societies as shadowy, all-powerful entities, reinforcing the narrative. Reflect on how these portrayals influence your views. Consider the role of fear in shaping these beliefs and how critical thinking can help navigate these complex narratives.

Reflect & Question: Media Influence

Critically evaluating the role of media in spreading conspiracy theories begins with understanding how traditional media outlets shape public perception. Newspapers, television, and radio have long been the gatekeepers of information, deciding which stories to highlight and how to present them. Sensational headlines and dramatic visuals often attract more viewers, which can lead to exaggerated or misleading coverage. Reflect on how these choices influence your understanding of events. Consider the impact of social media platforms and algorithms, prioritizing engaging content and often pushing conspiracy theories to the forefront. Algorithms designed to maximize user engagement can create echo chambers, where users are exposed primarily to content that reinforces their existing beliefs, making it harder to encounter dissenting views.

The broader implications of media influence on belief in conspiracy theories are profound. Sensationalism and misinformation can skew public opinion and behavior, leading to widespread distrust in authoritative sources. This erosion of trust can foster political and social movements built on misinformation, as seen with various anti-government and anti-science factions. Reflect on how media shapes these movements, questioning the balance between responsible reporting and the need for viewer engagement. How does sensationalism impact your perception of reality?

Exploring alternative explanations for the spread of conspiracy theories, consider cognitive biases and psychological factors. Human brains are wired to seek patterns and make sense of complex information, often leading to accepting simple but incorrect explanations. Social networks and group dynamics also play crucial roles, as people are more likely to believe information endorsed by their peers. Reflect on how these factors contribute to the proliferation of conspiracy theories. How do social networks reinforce your beliefs?

Questioning the motivations behind media coverage of conspiracy theories uncovers a complex web of profit motives, audience engagement, and editorial bias. Media outlets, driven by the need for high ratings and advertising revenue, might promote sensational stories to attract viewers. Reflect on how these profit motives shape the news you consume. Editorial bias and journalistic standards also influence how stories are reported. Question the integrity of the sources you rely on, considering the potential for bias and manipulation. How do these factors influence your trust in media?

REFERENCES AND ACKNOWLEDGMENTS

This book synthesizes insights from documentaries, podcasts, blogs, and other media through my own analysis. While I did not directly cite specific works, I've included a list of valuable resources for those interested in exploring these topics further.

Throughout the writing process, generative AI tools helped verify factual accuracy, supplementing the research in the listed sources.

References:

Britannica. (n.d.). *Conspiracy theory | Definition, examples, & facts.* Retrieved from https://www.britannica.com/topic/conspiracy-theory

Clarke, S. P., et al. (2020). *The history of conspiracy theory research: A review and analysis.* Oxford University Press. Retrieved from https://academic.oup.com/book/25369/chapter/192450613

Douglas, K. M., & Sutton, R. M. (2018). The psychology of conspiracy theories. *Psychological Science, 572(3).* Retrieved from https://www.ncbi.nlm.nih.gov/pmc/articles/PMC5724570/

Oxford Academic. (2020). *19 conspiracy theories in U.S. history.* Retrieved from https://academic.oup.com/book/25369/chapter/192461943

Grimes, D. R. (2021). How to disprove a conspiracy theory in 7 steps. *Scientific American.* Retrieved from https://www.scientificamerican.com/article/how-to-disprove-a-conspiracy-theory-in-7-steps/

Conceptually. (n.d.). *Occam's razor - Definition and examples.* Retrieved from https://conceptually.org/concepts/occams-razor

Southern Connecticut State University. (2022). *Fact checking - Critical thinking: Conspiracy theories, urban legends, and fake news.* Retrieved from https://libguides.southernct.edu/conspiracy/factchecking

van Prooijen, J. W., & van Lange, P. A. M. (2020). The role of cognitive biases in conspiracy beliefs. *Journal of Experimental Social Psychology, 12604.* Retrieved from https://onlinelibrary.wiley.com/doi/full/10.1111/joes.12604

Chua, B. (2023). What we know and still don't know about JFK's assassination. *Time.* Retrieved from https://time.com/6338396/jfk-assassination-conspiracy-culture/

Farid, H. (2010). A 3-D lighting and shadow analysis of the JFK Zapruder film. *Journal of Forensic Sciences, 12(4),* 303-309. Retrieved from https://farid.berkeley.edu/downloads/publications/tr10a.pdf

History.com. (2017). *What really happened at Roswell?* Retrieved from https://www.history.com/news/roswell-ufo-aliens-what-happened

Britannica. (n.d.). *Illuminati - Bavarian, enlightenment, conspiracy.* Retrieved from https://www.britannica.com/topic/illuminati-group-designation/Later-illuminati

National Security Archive. (2001). *Northwoods.pdf.* Retrieved from https://nsarchive2.gwu.edu/news/20010430/northwoods.pdf

History.com. (2020). *How "Deep Throat" took down Nixon from inside the FBI.* Retrieved from https://www.history.com/news/watergate-deep-throat-fbi-informant-nixon

NPR. (2019). *Poisoner in chief: The CIA's secret quest for mind control.* Retrieved from https://www.npr.org/2019/09/09/758989641/the-cias-secret-quest-for-mind-control-torture-lsd-and-a-poisoner-in-chief

History.com. (2020). *Bay of Pigs: Invasion, failure & Fidel Castro.* Retrieved from https://www.history.com/topics/cold-war/bay-of-pigs-invasion

9/11 Commission. (2004). *The 9/11 Commission Report.* Retrieved from https://www.9-11commission.gov/report/911Report.pdf

Wikipedia. (n.d.). *World Trade Center controlled demolition conspiracy theories.* Retrieved from https://en.wikipedia.org/wiki/World_Trade_Center_controlled_demolition_conspiracy_theories

Associated Press. (2020). *A timeline of the Jeffrey Epstein, Ghislaine Maxwell scandal.* Retrieved from https://apnews.com/article/epstein-maxwell-timeline-b9f15710fabb72 e8581c71e94acf513e

Scientific American. (2020). *State secrecy explains the origins of the "deep state" conspiracy theory.* Retrieved from https://www.scientificamerican.com/article/state-secrecy-explai ns-the-origins-of-the-deep-state-conspiracy-theory/

Wikipedia. (n.d.). *Moon landing conspiracy theories.* Retrieved from https://en.wikiped ia.org/wiki/Moon_landing_conspiracy_theories

University of California, Irvine. (2016). *Surveyed scientists debunk chemtrails conspiracy theory.* Retrieved from https://news.uci.edu/2016/08/12/surveyed-scientists-debunk-c hemtrails-conspiracy-theory/

Modern Diplomacy. (2023). *HAARP technology: Debunking conspiracy theories and understanding the science.* Retrieved from https://moderndiplomacy.eu/2023/02/27/haa rp-technology-debunking-conspiracy-theories-and-understanding-the-science/

Wikipedia. (n.d.). *Moon landing conspiracy theories in popular culture.* Retrieved from h ttps://en.wikipedia.org/wiki/Moon_landing_conspiracy_theories_in_popular_culture

Reuters. (2023). *How the JFK assassination transformed media coverage.* Retrieved from https://www.reuters.com/article/lifestyle/how-the-jfk-assassination-transformed -media-coverage-idUSBRE9AK11S/

Sage Journals. (2021). Panic, pizza and mainstreaming the alt-right: A social analysis. *Sociological Research Online.* Retrieved from https://journals.sagepub.com/doi/10.117 7/00113921211034896

NPR. (2022). *How Alex Jones mainstreamed conspiracy theories.* Retrieved from https://www.npr.org/2022/08/06/1115936712/how-alex-jones-helped-mainstr eam-conspiracy-theories-into-american-life

NCBI. (2023). The relationship between social media use and beliefs in conspiracy theories. *Journal of Medical Internet Research.* Retrieved from https://www.ncbi.nlm.nih .gov/pmc/articles/PMC8262430/

Study.com. (2021). *Cold War espionage: Spies, organizations & events.* Retrieved from https://study.com/academy/lesson/cold-war-spies-espionage.html

The Conversation. (2023). *Princess Diana: Why her death 25 years ago has sparked so many conspiracy theories.* Retrieved from https://theconversation.com/princess-diana-why-her-death-25-years-ago-has-sparked-so-many-conspiracy-theories-189088

Independent Institute. (n.d.). *Do Freedom of Information Act files prove FDR had foreknowledge of Pearl Harbor?* Retrieved from https://www.independent.org/issues/article.asp?id=408

CIA. (n.d.). *Project MK-ULTRA.* Retrieved from https://www.cia.gov/readingroom/document/06760269

Federal Reserve History. (n.d.). *The meeting at Jekyll Island.* Retrieved from https://www.federalreservehistory.org/essays/jekyll-island-conference

Federal Reserve History. (n.d.). *The Great Recession and its aftermath.* Retrieved from https://www.federalreservehistory.org/essays/great-recession-and-its-aftermath

Cointelegraph. (2023). *Who is the mysterious Bitcoin creator Satoshi Nakamoto?* Retrieved from https://cointelegraph.com/learn/who-is-satoshi-nakamoto-the-creator-of-bitcoin

Federal Reserve Board. (2022). *How does the Federal Reserve affect inflation and unemployment?* Retrieved from https://www.federalreserve.gov/faqs/money_12856.htm

Pharmaphorum. (2020). *A history of the pharmaceutical industry.* Retrieved from https://pharmaphorum.com/r-d/a_history_of_the_pharmaceutical_industry

Worldwide Cancer Research. (2023). *Could somebody be hiding the cure for cancer?* Retrieved from https://www.worldwidecancerresearch.org/information-and-impact/cancer-myths-and-questions/could-somebody-be-hiding-the-cure-for-cancer/

NCBI. (2010). The autism-vaccine story: Fiction and deception? *Journal of Immunology Research.* Retrieved from https://www.ncbi.nlm.nih.gov/pmc/articles/PMC2954080/

NCBI. (2012). Origins of HIV and the AIDS pandemic. *Journal of Medical Science.* Retrieved from https://www.ncbi.nlm.nih.gov/pmc/articles/PMC3234451/

Britannica. (n.d.). *Freemasonry - Definition, history, stages, lodges, & facts.* Retrieved from https://www.britannica.com/topic/Freemasonry

Bilderberg Meetings. (n.d.). *Bilderberg meeting.* Retrieved from http://www.bilderbergmeetings.org/

Study.com. (n.d.). *Skull and Bones Society - History & Overview*. Retrieved from https://study.com/academy/lesson/skull-bones-history-overview-order-322.html

History.com. (2021). *How America's first third party influenced politics*. Retrieved from https://www.history.com/news/third-party-politics-anti-masonic

van Prooijen, J. W., & van Lange, P. A. M. (2020). The role of cognitive biases in conspiracy beliefs. *Journal of Experimental Social Psychology, 12604*. Retrieved from https://onlinelibrary.wiley.com/doi/full/10.1111/joes.12604

Douglas, K. M., & Sutton, R. M. (2018). The psychology of conspiracy theories. *Psychological Science, 572(3)*. Retrieved from https://www.ncbi.nlm.nih.gov/pmc/articles/PMC5724570/

NCBI. (2023). The relationship between social media use and beliefs in conspiracy theories. *Journal of Medical Internet Research*. Retrieved from https://www.ncbi.nlm.nih.gov/pmc/articles/PMC8262430/

The Atlantic. (2016). Is Donald Trump a charismatic leader? *The Atlantic*. Retrieved from https://www.theatlantic.com/science/archive/2016/10/why-people-fall-for-charismatic-leaders/503906/

Parks, R. W. (2012). Rhetorical strategies of legitimation: The 9/11 commission's public inquiry process. *CORE*. Retrieved from https://core.ac.uk/download/1586637.pdf

Tiwari, B., & Singh, B. (2023). Impact of social media on Indian politics after Covid-19 pandemic. *International Journal of Research and Humanities, 3(3)*, 17. Retrieved from https://doi.org/10.55544/ijrah.3.3.17

Frontiers in Public Health. (2023). Analysis regarding the impact of "fake news" on the quality of life of the population in a region affected by earthquake activity: The case of Romania–Northern Oltenia. *Journal of Public Health Research*. Retrieved from https://doi.org/10.3389/fpubh.2023.1244564

OSRS Lab. (2022). *Disinformation explained: What you need to know & why it matters*. Retrieved from https://osrslab.com/disinformation-explained-what-you-need-to-know-why-it-matters/

Christopher Newport University. (1960). *U-2 spy plane incident*. Retrieved from https://cnu.libguides.com/psthe1960s/u2plane

Palatiello, A. (2014). Leveraged lending guidelines for asset-based lenders. *The Secured Lender, 70(10),* 44-46.

Stern, C., West, T. V., & Schmitt, P. G. (2013). The liberal illusion of uniqueness. *Psychological Science.* Retrieved from https://doi.org/10.1177/0956797613500796

CryptoTrade Signals. (2023). *The basics of cryptocurrency.* Retrieved from https://cryptotradesignals.live/article/article.php?article=the-basics-of-cryptocurrency&id=205687

Olshaker, J. S. (2003). Influenza. *Emergency Medicine Clinics of North America.* Retrieved from https://doi.org/10.1016/s0733-8627(03)00018-x

Mansyur, T. N., Abimulyani, Y., Siregar, N. S. A., & Kainde, Y. Y. (2023). Edukasi pencegahan HIV-AIDS dan mother to child transmission of HIV pada wanita usia subur dalam mendukung Indonesia bebas AIDS 2030. *Jurnal ABDIMAS-HIP Pengabdian Kepada Masyarakat.* Retrieved from https://doi.org/10.37402/abdimaship.vol4.iss2.251

Parks, R. W. (2012). Rhetorical strategies of legitimation: The 9/11 commission's public inquiry process. *CORE.* Retrieved from https://core.ac.uk/download/1586637.pdf

LEAF Grants. (2012). *LEAF grants come home. Washington Daily News.* Retrieved from https://www.thewashingtondailynews.com/2012/07/14/leaf-grants-come-home/

American History. (n.d.). *Exploring the top 10 events that defined the Vietnam War.* Retrieved from https://american-history.net/vietnam-war/the-vietnam-war-top-10-events/

Made in the USA
Las Vegas, NV
28 December 2024

15522054R00094